MEET THE AUTHOR

Laurie Rozakis, Ph.D.

Troll Associates

Interior Illustrations by: Yvette Banek

ISBN: 0-8167-2582-9

Printed in the United States of America.

10 9 8 7 6 5 4 3

CONTENTS

To the Teacher v

Beverly Cleary 8

Tomie dePaola 14

Jean Craighead George 20

Gail Gibbons 26

Virginia Hamilton 32

Arnold Lobel 38

Katherine Paterson 44

Bill Peet 50

Cynthia Rylant 56

Maurice Sendak 62

Dr. Seuss 68

Chris Van Allsburg 74

Laura Ingalls Wilder 80

Generic Activity Sheets 86

Meet the Author is designed to provide you with innovative ways to spark a love of fine literature, reinforce crucial writing and reading skills, and join literature with other areas of study. In-depth background materials, lively activities for teachers to lead in the classroom, and pleasurable independent activity sheets provide you with the means to expand your students' literary horizons with the finest children's books available.

Meet the Author includes material on thirteen popular children's writers: Beverly Cleary, Tomie dePaola, Jean Craighead George, Gail Gibbons, Virginia Hamilton, Arnold Lobel, Katherine Paterson, Bill Peet, Cynthia Rylant, Maurice Sendak, Dr. Seuss, Chris Van Allsburg, and Laura Ingalls Wilder. Each chapter opens with a biography of the author, including background information about the author's career in children's books. When you paraphrase this information for your students, you can use the humorous anecdotes and the author's own remarks to engage students' interest from the very start. This book also provides a picture of each author, which your students will surely be interested in seeing!

Each concise biography is followed by a list of the author's major works. With this list, you can easily recognize and locate his or her most celebrated or influential works. Next come short summaries of all the books included in the list of works. These summaries note when a book has been awarded a Newbery, Caldecott, or other major literary prize; whether a book begins a series; if a book uses a specific writing or illustrative technique; and so forth. To help you integrate these works into your curriculum, a wide variety of important pedagogical details have been noted, including, for example, an author's use of literary techniques such as a "frame story" and mathematical concepts such as set theory.

After you read through the summaries of an author's works and decide which books to present to your class, you will find a series of activities pertaining to that author—activities for the classroom and activity sheets for students to work on independently. These activities begin with a focus on the author's style, intent, and language, and provide you with many different ways to reinforce reading, writing, and speaking skills. There are four different activities involving poetry alone—haiku, lyric, narrative, and limerick—all elastic enough in format to be adaptable for any elementary-school students regardless of their grade level or reading skill. These different activities also give you a way to integrate material from other areas of study. For example, activities on Laura Ingalls Wilder and Gail Gibbons challenge students to sharpen their geography with map work; the activities included in the chapters on Jean Craighead George and Dr. Seuss explore science through a nature collection and a weather project respectively. As you will see, the authors in this book have also inspired ideas for activities in mathematics, art, and music. These activities are designed to be fun and creative! Whether students are writing a class story, presenting a puppet show, amassing a magical zoo, staging a variety show, performing a pantomime, or writing a post card, they will be entranced by the possibilities inherent in good literature.

The last section of the book provides eleven generic activity sheets, appropriate for use during any reading unit. You might use one of these activity sheets to discover students' abilities and interests, to challenge their imaginations, or to evaluate their progress. The activities give students opportunities to work independently, with partners, or in small groups. These activity sheets can also be used to reinforce skills taught in activities elsewhere in the book.

Meet the Author is sure to help you frame your lessons and have students clamoring to read more books by their favorite authors!

Photography Credits

The photographs featured in *Meet the Author* are the work of the following photographers:

Beverly Cleary (page 8) by Margaret Miller

Tomie dePaola (page 14) by Jon Gilbert Fox

Jean Craighead George (page 20) by Ellan Young Photography

Virginia Hamilton (page 32) by Skylight Studios

Arnold Lobel (page 38) by Ian Anderson

Katherine Paterson (page 44) by Jill Paton Walsh

Maurice Sendak (page 62) by Chris Callis

Dr. Seuss (page 68) by Czeslaw Czaplinski

Beverly Cleary

(BORN 1916)

"My life was exceptionally happy," Beverly (Bunn) Cleary has noted, describing the blissful childhood days she spent roaming through her parents' thirteen-room farmhouse and around "Yamhill," their Oregon farm. Cleary was only six years old when her happiness abruptly ended. Unable to make a living from their small farm, her parents rented the acreage and moved to the city. "I was confined to a city classroom full of strange children after a life of freedom and isolation on a farm," Cleary later wrote, describing her rage and sorrow. Adding to her anger was her difficulty in learning to read.

Beverly Cleary

Relegated to the lowest reading group, she felt disgraced by her slowness. "I wanted to read, but somehow could not. I wept at home while my mother tried to drill me on the dreaded word charts."

By second grade, Cleary had made progress, and by third grade, she had discovered that reading could be pleasurable. However, she was soon dissatisfied with the primers and simplified folk tales available to children in those days. By the fifth grade, Cleary had vowed to write fun books for young readers.

Her family's continuing financial hardships added to her determination to be a children's book author. "I was sent off to college not to catch a husband, as was the custom for young women of that time and place, but to become independent," she claimed. With her diploma from the University of California at Berkeley firmly in hand, Cleary won her independence by becoming a children's librarian. Her first stories came from her experiences running the Saturday-afternoon story hours. "I mentally told the stories to that remembered audience and wrote them down as I told them," she recalls. In 1940 she married Clarence Cleary, and the couple moved to Oakland, California. When World War II ended, she relinquished her position as post librarian at the Oakland Army Hospital and began to write in earnest. She credits her beginnings to the reams of typing paper she found in the linen closet. "Now I'll have to write a book," she remarked to her husband. "Why don't you?" he responded. "Because we never have any sharp pencils," she replied. The next day he came home with a pencil sharpener, and her career was launched!

Although she has won numerous awards, including the Newbery Medal in 1984 for *Dear Mr. Henshaw*, Cleary finds the most rewarding aspect of her career "the number of people who tell me of a child who didn't enjoy reading until my books came along."

Henry Huggins. Morrow, 1950.

Ellen Tebbits. Morrow, 1951.

Otis Spofford. Morrow, 1953.

Henry and Ribsy. Morrow, 1954.

Beezus and Ramona. Morrow, 1955.

The Luckiest Girl. Morrow, 1958.

Jean and Johnny. Morrow, 1959.

Ribsy. Morrow, 1964.

Ramona and Her Father. Morrow, 1977.

Ralph S. Mouse. Morrow, 1982.

Dear Mr. Henshaw. Morrow, 1983.

Ramona Forever. Morrow, 1984.

Muggie Maggie. Morrow, 1990.

Strider. Morrow, 1991.

ALL ABOUT THE BOOKS

Henry Huggins describes how eight-year-old Henry finds a stray dog ("Ribsy") at a drugstore and maneuvers to keep him.

Ellen Tebbits, lonely because her best friend has moved, finds a new friend in Austine when the two succeed in shedding their woolen underwear.

Otis Spofford "stirs up a little excitement" by throwing spitballs, chewing garlic and breathing on people, cutting a chunk from Ellen Tebbits's hair, and generally amusing his readers with his mischief.

Henry and Ribsy chronicles Henry's efforts to keep Ribsy out of trouble for two months. If Henry succeeds, he can accompany his father on a fishing trip.

Beezus and Ramona tells how polite eight-year-old Beezus (Beatrice) comes to accept her rambunctious four-year-old sister Ramona, after Ramona twice ruins Beezus's birthday cake.

The Luckiest Girl tells how Shelley Latham moves to California before she begins college, to live with her mother's old college roommate for a year. Shelley meets handsome Phil and tries to find out if he likes her.

Jean and Johnny describes Jean Jarrett's insecurity as she wonders what good-looking Johnny Chessler thinks of her.

Ribsy, which explores Ribsy's troubles when he is separated from Henry, is related entirely from the dog's viewpoint.

Ramona and Her Father shows how seven-year-old Ramona unsuccessfully tries to become a star to earn money for her unemployed father.

Ralph S. Mouse is the story of a dashing mouse who loses his cherished motorcycle but gains a sports car and the respect of his relatives.

Dear Mr. Henshaw tells how Leigh Botts, through an exchange of letters with a children's book writer, comes to terms with being the new kid in school, the disappearance of his dog Bandit, and, most important, his parents' divorce.

Ramona Forever describes how Ramona matures in the face of three big changes: her mother's pregnancy, her newfound freedom, and her aunt's marriage.

Muggie Maggie tells how fourth-grader Maggie refuses to learn cursive writing, deciding it is unnecessary. When she finally tries cursive, "Maggie" comes out "Muggie." Her teacher ingeniously teaches Maggie cursive writing.

Strider, a sequel to *Dear Mr. Henshaw*, chronicles how Leigh Botts becomes close to Strider, the abandoned dog he rescues and adopts.

──────────────────────────── **ACTIVITIES** ────────────────────────────

Face to Face Cleary's characters—including Henry Huggins, Ellen Tebbits, Otis Spofford, Ribsy, and Ralph S. Mouse—enjoy wacky, wild adventures. Invite each student to select any one character from any of Cleary's books. Have students list their character's personality traits, using a book in which the character appears as a reference. Then arrange students in pairs, making sure the students in each pair have chosen different characters. Have pairs create a skit showing an adventure between their characters. Let students perform their skits for the class.

Don't Turn That Dial! The Ramona books provide the themes for a ten-part television series. Have students write and perform an episode suitable for inclusion in the series. The episode can derive directly from one of the Ramona books or it may be a new adventure. Write the script together as a class. Then divide the class into small groups to work on acting, costumes, scenery, props, and lighting. When students are ready, they can perform their episode for another class, their parents, or community members. Your school media specialist or a parent volunteer can videotape the episode so students can view it later.

The Invention Convention In *Dear Mr. Henshaw*, Leigh Botts rigs a burglar alarm in his lunch box to stop thieves from stealing his lunch. Have students design and build their own unusual inventions. Suggest that students begin by deciding on their invention's purpose. Then have them build their inventions from commonplace materials such as foil, string, cardboard tubes, and found objects. More advanced students might want to use batteries and create moving parts. Gather all the inventions for display in an "Invention Convention."

Stock Your Shelves Beverly Cleary wanted to write children's books because she didn't like the ones that were available to her as a child. Today, children have a much greater range of interesting reading choices than Cleary did. Have students create their own personal libraries by selecting twenty-five books they would like to own. These books can include novels such as Cleary's works, nonfiction books, and reference texts. Begin by brainstorming as a class a list of books that students especially liked reading or have heard others talk about. Then have each student select the twenty-five books for his or her personal library and write a one-sentence reason for each choice. Finally, have students share their lists and their rationales.

Announcing . . .

In *Dear Mr. Henshaw*, Leigh Botts writes letters to his favorite author. On the lines below, write a letter to *your* favorite author, inviting him or her to speak at your school. Explain why you admire the author and why you want him or her to speak to your classmates.

Beverly Cleary

Arnold Lobel

Laura Ingalls Wilder

Dr. Seuss

Maurice Sendak

Bill Peet

Tomie dePaola

Katherine Paterson

Gail Gibbons

Jean Craighead George

Virginia Hamilton

Chris Van Allsburg

Dear Mr. Henshaw
Beverly Cleary

Q Is for Cat?

In one of her many adventures, Ramona drew her own personalized initial in wet cement. She turned a Q (for Quimby) into a cat. You wouldn't write in wet cement, but you *can* create personalized initials for your own name.

In the space below, write the first letters of your first name, middle name (if you have one), and last name. Then turn your initials into your own personal creations.

Beezus and Ramona
Ramona and Her Father
Ramona Forever
Beverly Cleary

Tomie dePaola

[de-POW-1a] (BORN 1934)

When he was six years old, Tomie dePaola struck a deal with his art teacher: he would draw the Pilgrim she demanded if she would then allow him to draw whatever he wished. When he completed the picture he really wanted to draw, his art teacher asked for it. He refused, saying, "No, I'm saving it to sell." And so began dePaola's career as an illustrator of children's books. He has been astonishingly successful in selling his work to the children's book industry—to date he has illustrated more than eighty children's books by other authors, and he has written and illustrated more than sixty books of his own.

Tomie dePaola

The son of an Italian father and Irish mother, dePaola was sandwiched between an older brother and two younger sisters in a household devoted to cooking good meals. His family, in fact, had a great influence on the writing he later did for children; food and Italian culture were subjects he returned to again and again. After completing high school in his hometown of Meriden, Connecticut, dePaola earned his Bachelor of Fine Arts degree from Pratt Institute in Brooklyn, New York. After a stint as a free-lance illustrator of Christmas cards, theater designs, and religious art, dePaola taught art at Newton College of the Sacred Heart in Newton, Massachusetts. In 1966 he entered the California College of Arts and Crafts, where he earned his Master of Fine Arts degree three years later. Among his classmates was Arnold Lobel, another children's book author and illustrator who became well known (especially for his series of *Frog and Toad* books). Soon after, dePaola pursued his doctoral course work at San Francisco's Lone Mountain College.

He returned to the East Coast to teach art, speech, and theater at a number of colleges and to pursue his long-standing dream of writing and illustrating children's books. Some of his inspiration comes from classical art. The classical influence is particularly strong in *Francis: the Poor Man of Assisi*, which dePaola wrote and illustrated in 1982 to honor the 800th anniversary of the birth of Saint Francis of Assisi. DePaola drew inspiration for this book's illustrations from the frescoes of Cimabue and Simone Martini in the Basilica of San Francesco in Assisi, which he visited first in 1956 and again in 1978. Legends and folk tales also play a part in dePaola's imagination. The inspiration for *Strega Nona*, for instance, came from his research of the rice-pot stories of India.

Charlie Needs a Cloak. Simon & Schuster, 1974.

Strega Nona. Simon & Schuster, 1975.

Helga's Dowry: A Troll Love Story. Harcourt Brace Jovanovich, 1977.

The Clown of God: An Old Story. Harcourt Brace Jovanovich, 1978.

Bill and Pete. Putnam, 1978.

Big Anthony and the Magic Ring. Harcourt Brace Jovanovich, 1979.

The Lady of Guadalupe. Holiday House, 1980.

The Legend of Old Befana. Harcourt Brace Jovanovich, 1980.

Strega Nona's Magic Lessons. Harcourt Brace Jovanovich, 1982.

Merry Christmas, Strega Nona. Harcourt Brace Jovanovich, 1986.

Bill and Pete Go Down the Nile. Putnam, 1987.

Tomie dePaola's Book of Bible Stories. Putnam, 1990.

Bonjour, Mr. Satie. Putnam, 1991.

ALL ABOUT THE BOOKS

Charlie Needs a Cloak explains how the shepherd shears his sheep, spins the wool, and weaves and dyes the cloth to make his beautiful cloak.

Strega Nona, the 1975 Caldecott Honor Book, describes how Big Anthony cannot stop Strega Nona's magic pasta pot from filling the town with pasta. As punishment, Big Anthony must eat all the pasta.

Helga's Dowry: A Troll Love Story is about the beautiful but poor troll Helga, who uses magic to acquire enough material possessions for a dowry, but winds up acquiring independence and forsaking the troll she wished to marry.

The Clown of God: An Old Story relates how the juggler Giovanni miraculously causes a statue of the Christ child to smile.

Bill and Pete describes how Bill Everett, a talking crocodile, buys Pete, a talking bird, to use as his toothbrush.

Big Anthony and the Magic Ring tells how Big Anthony uses Strega Nona's magic ring to become handsome, and is chased by enamored village women.

The Lady of Guadalupe recounts the legend of how the Virgin Mary became the patron saint of Mexico.

The Legend of Old Befana tells how Befana brings the Christ child baked treats and a broom to sweep his nursery. Every year after that, for the Feast of Kings, Befana delivers goodies to children and sweeps their rooms clean.

Strega Nona's Magic Lessons explains how Bambolina and Strega Nona get the best of Big Anthony when he attempts to misuse magic.

Merry Christmas, Strega Nona is about Strega Nona's Christmas feast, which the townspeople give her because Big Anthony has forgotten the ingredients.

Bill and Pete Go Down the Nile follows Pete and Bill on a class trip to study Egyptian artifacts. Pete foils the bad guy they encounter on the trip.

Tomie dePaola's Book of Bible Stories contains 128 pages of dePaola's interpretations of well-loved Bible stories.

Bonjour, Mr. Satie relates the adventures of Mr. Satie, a cat, and his friend, the mouse Fortie. Together, the pair travel through Paris in the 1920s, where they meet with various famous animal friends, including Pablo, a painter.

The Feast of dePaola   Often dePaola's books concern food and feasting. Have students plan and prepare a simplified feast of the goodies featured in the dePaola books they have read. The feast could be a pasta party in honor of the Strega Nona books, or a smorgasbord of baked goods that commemorate Befana. The activity can be expanded to feature such easy-to-prepare foods as gelatin, instant pudding, raw vegetables, fruit muffins, and so forth. As students plan and prepare their feast, incorporate work with ingredient measurement and discussion of hygiene (washing hands and foods before eating).

A Class Folk Tale   Many of dePaola's most beloved stories are in the folklore tradition. Explain to students what a folk tale is. It is a short story with a quick introduction of a problem, a few events (often three), and a quick resolution. The characters in a folk tale are usually one-dimensional and often represent a quality such as evil or goodness. A folk tale is passed around a particular group of people, often for many generations. DePaola's stories very often echo Italian folklore. To show students the timeless appeal of folklore, have the class create its own folk tale. Arrange students in a circle and discuss events from school that might make a memorable story for people to pass on and on. To help students generate ideas, use prompts such as, "Remember the time that . . . ," "What did you think when . . . ," "What do you recall about your first day in my class?" To begin the story, say, "Once upon a time in my class . . . ." Have each student in turn add a line to the story until everyone has had a chance and the story is complete. Transcribe the story on large paper as students speak, or tape-record it so that later they can hear their own voices telling the story.

Artist for a Day   Select a dePaola book the students have not yet read. Write the words from each page on large sheets of poster board and set aside. Then read the book aloud several times, but do not show the illustrations. Take out the poster board with the story's words. Arrange students in groups, one per page, and have them illustrate the book. After students have finished, staple the book together and read it to the class. Then reread the book and show them dePaola's illustrations. Compare and contrast the class's work to dePaola's. Consider accuracy of clothes and setting, and how the pictures help to tell the story.

A Special Day   Holidays are the core of many of dePaola's books. Invite the students to invent a holiday of their own, celebrating something the entire class decides is special. Begin by having the class brainstorm some ideas for their holiday. Then work together to select the day, give it a name, and have the class decide an appropriate way to celebrate the day. Finally, stage the celebration.

I Wish . . .

Make believe you have Strega Nona's magic ring. What would you wish for? Write your wish on the lines. Then draw a picture of your wish come true.

If I had Strega Nona's magic ring, I would wish _____

_____

_____.

A Big Trip

Bill and Pete, the traveling chums from *Bill and Pete Go Down the Nile*, want you to go with them on a trip. Where to? Write where you decide to go on the line below. Then draw pictures of all the things you would take with you on your trip.

I am going to _____.

Bill and Pete Go Down the Nile
Tomie dePaola

Jean Craighead George

(BORN 1919)

Jean Craighead George's fascination with nature is reflected in her books. While gathering material for *Water Sky*, for instance, she spent six weeks on the sea ice off Barrow, Alaska—where the temperature was more than thirty degrees below zero! She even brings nature into her home: she and her family have raised more than 150 wild animals and then returned them to their natural settings.

There is no doubt that some of her interest in nature comes from her childhood. The daughter of a zoologist, George was early acquainted with birds and animals, many of which roamed freely around her parents' home. For recreation, the family hiked through woods and swamplands. After completing her elementary and secondary education in her hometown of Washington, D.C., George earned a B.A. degree from Pennsylvania State University, where she majored in science. Her graduate work was in art, at Louisiana State University and the University of Michigan.

Soon after completing her education, she married John L. George. Jean and John wrote six books together, beginning with *Vulpes,*

Jean Craighead George

the Red Fox, which Jean also illustrated. Then Jean Craighead George began to write alone.

In addition to writing and illustrating books for children, she has contributed to a number of periodicals, having worked as a reporter for the International News Service (1942–44), *The Washington Post* (1944–46), and *Reader's Digest* (1974–82), and as a staff writer and art director for *Pageant* magazine. She has also been a free-lance artist. In many instances, George has produced a nonfiction article that spawned a children's fictional work. "The Sociable Sea Gull," for example, which she wrote for *National Geographic*, sparked her to write *Gull Number 737*, a novel about a father and son whose recordings of gulls' calls draw birds away from the paths of oncoming airplanes.

According to Flo Krall of *Western American Literature*, Jean Craighead George is "a woman who seems not to find the words 'despair' or 'loneliness' in her vocabulary, a woman who fashioned her life after the black wolf."

Dipper of Copper Creek. Dutton, 1956.

The Hole in the Tree. Dutton, 1957.

Snow Tracks. Dutton, 1958.

My Side of the Mountain. Dutton, 1959.

The Summer of the Falcon. Crowell, 1962.

Gull Number 737. Crowell, 1964.

Spring Comes to the Ocean. Crowell, 1965.

Hold Zero! Crowell, 1966.

Coyote in Manhattan. Crowell, 1968.

Julie of the Wolves. Harper, 1972.

River Rats, Inc. Dutton, 1979.

The Cry of the Crow. Harper, 1980.

Journey Inward. Dutton, 1982.

How to Talk to Your Animals. Harcourt Brace Jovanovich, 1985.

One Day in the Tropical Rain Forest. Harper, 1990.

ALL ABOUT THE BOOKS

Dipper of Copper Creek, co-authored by John George, provides facts about the life cycle of the water ouzel as it describes Doug Smith's desire for independence.

The Hole in the Tree accompanies Scott and Paula Gordon as they watch a bark beetle and a woodpecker make a hole in an old apple tree.

Snow Tracks parallels the trails left in the snow by the boy Trapper and by animals searching for food and shelter.

My Side of the Mountain, a Newbery Honor Book, tells how young Sam Gribley survives in the wilderness for a year.

The Summer of the Falcon shows how June Pritchard learns self-discipline as she trains a falcon.

Gull Number 737 tells how Luke Rivers and his father use a tape of gulls' distress calls to lure birds away from the paths of airplanes.

Spring Comes to the Ocean describes twelve ocean creatures' responses to the change of seasons in the Atlantic and Pacific.

Hold Zero! focuses on teenagers Steve and Craig Sutton's interest in rockets.

Coyote in Manhattan explains how Tenny Harkness releases a coyote into New York, and how the coyote takes up residence in Central Park.

Julie of the Wolves, the 1973 Newbery Medal Winner, is the story of an Eskimo girl, Julie Edward Miyaz Kapugen, who survives on the Alaskan tundra through self-reliance and intelligence.

River Rats, Inc. tells how Joe Zero and Crowbar Flood teach a wild mute to speak. In turn, the mute, whom they call the Lizard Boy, teaches them survival skills.

The Cry of the Crow tells about May Tressel's heart-wrenching decision to shoot her crow after it attacks her brother.

Journey Inward, Jean Craighead George's autobiography, describes her divorce, her experiences as a single parent, her work as a writer, and her love of nature.

How to Talk to Your Animals outlines animals' communication patterns and encourages humans to watch animals and respond to them by imitating their sounds.

One Day in the Tropical Rain Forest combines an explanation of the life cycle of the rain forest with the story of a young Indian boy saving his home, the rain forest, from destruction. The boy finds a rare butterfly that a rich man covets. The rich man names the butterfly after his granddaughter and donates enough money to save the rain forest from the bulldozers.

―――――――――――――――――――――――――― **ACTIVITIES** ――――――――――――――――――――――――――

Experience Nature Take students on a brief walk through a park, wooded area, nature preserve, lake region, marsh, or ocean area. On the walk, have them gather a few leaves, grasses, shells, flowers, abandoned nests, seed pods, and so forth. In place of a class walk, you can have students bring in objects they have collected on their own excursions in nature. Have each student mount his or her objects on a large poster board with glue or tape. Direct students to look up their objects in an encyclopedia, science book, or other reference text and label each object with its common and technical name, natural habitat, and life cycle. Display the posters around the classroom.

"Help Save the Animal" Campaign Eagles, cheetahs, pandas, whales, grizzly and polar bears, tigers, swans, and wolves are just a few of the animals in danger of extinction. First discuss endangered species with students and have the class develop a list of such creatures. Then arrange students in groups of three to four. Have each group select an endangered animal and design a campaign to help ensure its survival. Campaign messages should give the reasons why the animal is endangered. Encourage students to do research. Suggest that students experiment with various media, including posters, television and radio commercials, buttons, fliers, print ads, and pamphlets in formulating their campaign.

Express Yourself Explore with students how nature deeply moves many people. An unspoiled field of flowers, a lake, or a mountain, for example, give many people great joy. Some people express their feelings about nature in poetry. Have students write narrative or lyric poems about a positive experience they have had with nature. First explain to students that narrative poems tell a story in poetry—with events, characters, and a setting—and often use rhyme. Tell them that lyric poems, in contrast, present an experience or single effect without telling a full story. Lyric poems often express the poet's feelings and are highly musical. Suggest that students begin their poems with a cluster diagram centered around a specific experience with nature. Then direct them to select from these words to begin their rough draft. When students have completed their final drafts, they may wish to illustrate their poems, and create a class book or post them on the class bulletin board.

You Be the Judge Many people want to help protect the environment but are often not in agreement about what must be done. Begin by exploring with students different things they can do as individuals and in small groups to preserve nature and its inhabitants. They may say that they can pick up garbage; recycle plastic, glass, metal, and paper; feed wild creatures in the winter and in times of famine; and avoid using aerosol sprays that destroy the ozone layer. Then have small groups create simple plans to help preserve the environment. Have each group present its plan to the class in the form of a panel discussion. After all the groups have spoken, have the class vote on the plan they think will be the most successful. Finally, have students implement that plan. You might want to set up a chart to provide a visual account of students' progress.

Dear Diary . . . with a Difference!

In *One Day in the Tropical Rain Forest*, a young boy saves the rain forest when he finds a rare butterfly. Imagine that you are the young boy in the story. Write a diary entry describing a day in your life. Include information about your surroundings, your family, your fears, and your triumphs. Write your entry on the lines provided below.

_____

_____

_____

_____

_____

_____

_____

_____

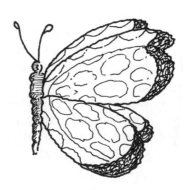

One Day in the Tropical Rain Forest
Jean Craighead George

What Would *You* Take Along?

In *Julie of the Wolves,* the Eskimo girl Julie Kapugen learns to survive on the Alaskan tundra. In *River Rats, Inc.,* Joe Zero and Crowbar Flood learn to survive in the Grand Canyon. All of these characters have only the bare necessities. Imagine that *you* were marooned on a desert island. You can take only ten things with you. What things would you take—and why? List the ten items you would take to your desert island and write a sentence to explain each choice.

Item #1 _____

_____

Item #2 _____

_____

Item #3 _____

_____

Item #4 _____

_____

Item #5 _____

_____

Item #6 _____

_____

Item #7 _____

_____

Item #8 _____

_____

Item #9 _____

_____

Item #10 _____

_____

Julie of the Wolves
Jean Craighead George

Gail Gibbons

(BORN 1944)

In fewer than ten years, Gail Gibbons has produced over thirty books for children. The quality of her output is as notable as its quantity. Whether writing and illustrating picture or board books for very young children or books for middle-grade students, Gibbons's work shows her talent for putting facts into an understandable and attractive format for young readers.

Her books are especially acclaimed for their illustrations. Her watercolors, for example, display a primitivism young readers like. She varies her brushstrokes, making some broken and some bold, to create arresting tableaux. Colors are especially important to her work. The pictures in *The Post Office Book*, for instance, depict the bustle and efficiency of the U.S. Post Office in patriotic red, white, and blue.

The daughter of a tool-and-die designer, Gail Gibbons (born Gail George) spent her childhood in the Illinois towns of Oak Park, Palos Heights, and Blue Island. In 1967 she received her Bachelor of Fine Arts degree in graphic design from the University of Illinois. "I became interested in writing children's books when in college," Gibbons recalled, but she did not pursue a vocation of her own in the field for many years.

After college, Gibbons worked as a graphic artist for an Illinois television station. She was responsible for producing on-the-air graphics, animation, and printed promotional material. Next she spent several years doing free-lance animation for NBC in Chicago. In 1970 she and her husband Glenn Gibbons, whom she had married while they were students in college, moved to New York City. After spending two years doing artwork for NBC's children's show "Take a Giant Step," Gibbons's interest in developing her own children's books intensified. In 1972, after her husband died in an accident, Gibbons changed her professional course. "I decided to reduce my work load to put my life back into some kind of order," she noted, and "began getting involved in my artwork again, on a free-lance basis." She contacted a literary agent, who encouraged her to use her writing and drawing abilities to teach young children about set theory (problem-solving that involves sets, or groups, of objects or ideas). The result was her first book, *Willy and His Wheel Wagon* (1975).

In 1976 Gibbons married Kent Ancliffe. She credits her stepchildren with giving her interesting ideas for books, and also notes that her home in Corinth, Vermont, has played a key role in her work. "We live in a rural farm area where maple sugaring is done and other homespun activities take place," she remarked. These pastimes sparked *The Missing Maple Syrup Sap Mystery* (1979).

Gail Gibbons

Clocks and How They Go. Crowell, 1979.

Trucks. Crowell, 1981.

The Post Office Book. Crowell, 1982.

New Road! Crowell, 1983.

Thanksgiving Day. Holiday House, 1983.

The Department Store. Crowell, 1984.

Fill It Up! All About Service Stations. Crowell, 1985.

Lights! Camera! Action! How a Movie Is Made. Crowell, 1985.

The Milk Makers. Macmillan, 1985.

From Path to Highway: The Story of the Boston Post Road.
  Crowell, 1986.

Up Goes the Skyscraper. Macmillan, 1986.

Zoo. Crowell, 1987.

Dinosaurs. Holiday House, 1987.

Beacons of Light: Lighthouses. Morrow, 1990.

How a House Is Built. Holiday House, 1990.

The Puffins Are Back. Harper, 1991.

Surrounded by Sea: Life in a New England Fishing Village.
  Little, Brown, 1991.

ALL ABOUT THE BOOKS

Clocks and How They Go uses bright, bold pictures to explain to
  the very young reader the basic mechanism behind clocks.

Trucks provides a simple text and well-labeled illustrations to show
  a variety of trucks and what they do.

The Post Office Book describes the activities performed by postal
  employees, including sorting mail, loading it into trucks and
  planes, and delivering. The illustrations are bright and busy.

New Road! explores the process of constructing a road.

Thanksgiving Day uses a simple text and colorful illustrations to
  show the origins of Thanksgiving and the different ways it is
  celebrated now.

The Department Store features different people and activities in a
  department store. Included are customers, salespeople, stockroom
  workers, and display artists.

Fill It Up! All About Service Stations presents a detailed description of what goes on in a service station. Illustrations help to explain how a hydraulic lift works and where gasoline is stored.

Lights! Camera! Action! How a Movie Is Made details the various responsibilities the task entails.

The Milk Makers follows the production of milk from the cow to the store. The book tells what cows eat, how their four stomachs work, and how they are milked.

From Path to Highway: The Story of the Boston Post Road chronicles the development of the Boston Post Road from an Indian trail into a highway.

Zoo uses colorful pictures and a clear text to explain the jobs people have at the zoo. Included, for example, is information on how keepers monitor animals and plan special exhibits.

Dinosaurs highlights fourteen different dinosaurs, including Tyrannosaurus rex and Apatosaurus.

Beacons of Light: Lighthouses uses evocative watercolors to trace the history of lighthouses around the country and shows how lighthouse technology has changed over the years.

How a House Is Built, aimed at preschoolers to grade 3, describes the process by which a house is erected.

Up Goes the Skyscraper traces the construction of a skyscraper from the clearing of the construction site to the day the tenants move in.

The Puffins Are Back describes how scientists help restore the world's puffin population by seeding a small New England island with puffins from Newfoundland.

Surrounded by Sea: Life in a New England Fishing Village tells about life in a small fishing village off the coast of Maine. Gibbons describes how the villagers dig for clams, trap lobsters, and maintain their many different kinds of fishing boats and nets.

─────────────────── **ACTIVITIES** ───────────────────

Truckin' Read Gibbons's *Trucks* to students. Then ask the class to talk about trucks. Remind students what they have read about trucks and have them make a list of all the different kinds they can find out about. Encourage them to use encyclopedias or other research materials.

Working from this list, ask students to bring in pictures of trucks from magazines. The following day, have the class create its own truck book. Working from their pictures, have each student prepare a page with a truck, its name, and one sentence describing its function. Gather the pages together and then read the book to the class, showing each page as you do so.

A Magical Modern Zoo Gibbons's *Zoo* describes a typical day at the zoo. Read the book to students. Then explain that the first zoos were collections of animals displayed in cages, but many of today's zoos provide natural habitats for animals and separate them by ditches or water too wide for the animals—and people!—to cross. In modern zoos, animals are allowed to roam over large, open-air ranges. Often, animals of different species are exhibited together, sharing the same natural environment that they would share in the wild.

Tell students they are going to create their own Magical Modern Zoo. Have them bring in any stuffed animal they wish, even a mythical creature like a unicorn or an extinct one like a dinosaur. Have students decide which animals they think would be happy living together and which would have to live alone. Then have groups of students create "environments" for their animals. They can use paper, clay, toys, and so forth to create their areas. They may wish to design real environments, such as an African plain, or make mythical places. When all the exhibits are finished, invite others to visit the zoo. Assign students the jobs Gibbons describes, such as assisting "sick" animals, collecting tickets, and cleaning up.

From Here to There In *From Path to Highway: The Story of the Boston Post Road*, Gibbons traces the path of the road. Using a large map of the United States, have volunteers point out well-known cities, such as state capitals and places they might have visited. Ask students to come to the map and use their fingers to trace a way to go from their town to one of these places. You might also want to discuss different types of roads, from obscure paths to highways.

Next, have students draw a map of the school building. When everyone is finished, have them draw on their maps the path they take from the outside of the building to the classroom. Share the maps by creating a bulletin-board display.

Voom Voom Vehicle! Gibbons shows several commonplace vehicles and explains how they function. Invite your students to explore a less common conveyance. Have them build their own class vehicle and then explain what *it* can do. From a grocery store, obtain half a dozen large boxes. Have students contribute various containers, such as paper towel and toilet paper tubes and shoe and gift boxes. Then have students work together on their creation. You can staple or glue the materials. Have students paint, color, and decorate their vehicle and then explain what it can do. Students might also want to get into the vehicle to demonstrate its capabilities.

The Tallest Building in the World

Gail Gibbons wrote about how skyscrapers are built. If you were making a skyscraper, what would it look like? In the space below, draw your own skyscraper. Then draw some of the smaller buildings around it.

My skyscraper is so tall that _____

_____.

Up Goes the Skyscraper
Gail Gibbons

How Does It Work?

Gail Gibbons's books tell how things work. Think of something you know how to do—brush your teeth, set the table, make your bed. Pick one of these things and, in the space below, draw each step you take to do it. Write numbers under each step so people can follow your pictures. Then let a friend read your paper. See if your friend can follow your steps.

Virginia Hamilton

(BORN 1936)

The winner of many prestigious book awards, including the National Book award and the Newbery Medal, Virginia Hamilton was surrounded by storytellers from birth. "My own mother could take a slice of fiction floating around the family and polish it into a saga," she claimed. Hamilton's books reflect her personality as well as her heritage. "What personal self I have is in my books," she has noted. "Everything that might become neurotic or personally problematic I put into a narrative. My stories are little pieces of me."

The youngest of five children, Hamilton grew up in Yellow Springs, Ohio, a former station of the Underground Railroad. Her maternal grandfather had escaped from slavery to settle in Yellow Springs, eventually buying land and nurturing his large, close family. Hamilton was educated at a small country school and was the only black girl in her class until the seventh grade. Although she did well in her classes, she felt her education was limited and longed to leave Yellow Springs. Her chance came when her high school teacher arranged for a five-year college scholarship. Even with her tuition paid, Hamilton could not afford to board at school, so she chose nearby Antioch College. On the advice of her teachers, she spent summers in New York, working, as she said, at "every source of

Virginia Hamilton

occupation imaginable, from singer to bookkeeper." After completing her B.A. in 1955, she decided to move to New York to try her hand at writing fiction.

She worked hard at her writing, but nothing was accepted for publication for a long time. On the basis of her samples, however, she was admitted to a select writing course at The New School. Her teacher, Hiram Hayden, one of the founders of Atheneum publishers, tried to help her publish a novel, but it too was rejected. Several years later she submitted a story that she had written as a student to the children's book department at Macmillan. The story evolved into *Zeely*, her first book. On its publication in 1967, the book received good reviews, and Hamilton's career was launched.

In recent years, Virginia Hamilton has been especially interested in delving into the black experience in America. *The People Could Fly: American Black Folktales*, published in 1985, is perhaps the most obvious example of her pursuit of the African-American heritage; this book contains 24 stories that trace the evolution of the African-American folk tale. "There are themes in my writing that are strains through the whole of black history," Hamilton notes. "Perhaps some day when I've written my last book, there will stand the whole of the black experience in white America as I see it."

Zeely. Macmillan, 1967.

The House of Dies Drear. Macmillan, 1968.

The Time-Ago Tales of Jahdu. Macmillan, 1969.

The Planet of Junior Brown. Collier, 1971.

W. E. B. Du Bois: A Biography. Crowell, 1972.

Time-Ago Lost: More Tales of Jahdu. Macmillan, 1973.

M. C. Higgins, the Great. Macmillan, 1974.

Paul Robeson: The Life and Times of a Free Black Man. Harper, 1974.

Arilla Sun Down. Greenwillow, 1976.

Justice and Her Brothers. Greenwillow, 1978.

Sweet Whispers, Brother Rush. Philomel, 1982.

The Magical Adventures of Pretty Pearl. Harper, 1983.

Willie Bea and the Time the Martians Landed. Greenwillow, 1983.

Junius Over Far. Harper, 1985.

A White Romance. Putnam, 1987.

The Mystery of Drear House. Greenwillow, 1987.

ALL ABOUT THE BOOKS

Zeely is about how a young girl named Elizabeth Perry, also called "Geeder," comes to self-realization after she encounters a majestic young black woman. Geeder imagines that the young woman is a Watusi queen enslaved by her cruel father to oversee his prize hogs.

The House of Dies Drear, winner of the Edgar Allan Poe Award for the best juvenile mystery of 1969, is a mystery that incorporates information about the Underground Railroad.

The Time-Ago Tales of Jahdu, a frame story, weaves allegorical tales of Sweetdream, Nightmare, Trouble, and other fantasy characters.

The Planet of Junior Brown describes how Junior is helped by his friends when he gradually loses his hold on reality.

W. E. B. Du Bois: A Biography chronicles the life of the black scholar, poet, civil rights leader, and teacher.

Time-Ago Lost: More Tales of Jahdu incorporates African tradition and mythology and Chinese cosmology to create another set of folktales.

M. C. Higgins, the Great, the 1975 Newbery winner and 1976 National Book Award winner, describes a family struggling to protect their home and environment from strip miners.

Paul Robeson: The Life and Times of a Free Black Man is a biography of the times as well as the man. Photographs are included.

Arilla Sun Down is about children of black–Native American intermarriage who try to discover where they belong in American society.

Justice and Her Brothers, the first book in a trilogy, focuses on four children with powers that allow them to mind-travel into the future.

Sweet Whispers, Brother Rush, a Newbery Honor Book, explores mental retardation and lupus, an inherited disease.

The Magical Adventures of Pretty Pearl describes a child god who leaves Africa to travel to Civil War America and eventually assume human form.

Willie Bea and the Time the Martians Landed, set on Halloween, 1938, takes off from Orson Welles's broadcast of "The War of the Worlds."

Junius Over Far, recommended for mature readers, focuses on the relationship of Junius Rawlings and his paternal grandfather.

A White Romance explores how track and running bond two students who come from very different backgrounds.

The Mystery of Drear House is the sequel to *The House of Dies Drear.*

ACTIVITIES

Celebrate Our Heritage Many of Virginia Hamilton's novels celebrate the heritage of black and Native Americans. Explore with students how American culture is unique because so many different nationalities combine to create it. You may wish to discuss the reopening of Ellis Island, the New York City immigration center. Many Americans contributed funds for its restoration; and for the displays at the center, many donated clothing, household goods, books, playthings, tools, and ornaments that they had brought with them from their birth lands when they immigrated. Ask volunteers to describe briefly customs unique to their backgrounds, such as special foods or holiday celebrations. Create a Cultural Awareness Day by having students bring in some token of their heritage: a doll in the native costume of one of their ancestors, an article of clothing or a household object from the "Old Country," or a letter written in the language of their ancestors. Those who enjoy cooking might want to bring in a dish unique to their ethnic group for others to taste. Create a display of these items for the class to share.

Snapshot of the Past Ask students to create an oral history of their oldest relative, friend, or neighbor. Suggest that students begin by working in small groups to write ten to fifteen questions to use in their interviews. Questions might include "What was school like when you were my age?" "What did you do in your leisure time?" and "What is the main difference between your childhood and mine?" Students can transcribe the answers or use a tape recorder. Encourage students to ask the people they interview for a photograph to accompany the transcript or tape. When everyone has completed the project, play the tapes for the class to share. You might want to set up an oral history corner in the classroom or school library.

Greatness Earned In addition to fiction, Virginia Hamilton wrote biographies of great Americans, including W. E. B. Du Bois and Paul Robeson. Suggest that students research the life of a great American, such as Lucretia Mott, George Washington Carver, or Chief Joseph. In their reports, have students trace the person's life and achievements. Encourage students to include a bibliography. If necessary, you might incorporate a lesson on bibliographic form. Have students share their papers by reading them to the class and answering classmates' questions afterward.

The War of the Worlds On October 31, 1938, Orson Welles's broadcast "The War of the Worlds" led some Americans to believe that Martians had invaded the United States. Virginia Hamilton built her novel *Willie Bea and the Time the Martians Landed* around this event. Have students write and perform their own radio theater. You might want to begin by playing a recording of Welles's famous broadcast, of the "Shadow" series, or of any other example of classic radio theater. Then, as a class, outline a play, building the action around an invasion from outer space or any other dramatic occurrence. Encourage students to work in small groups to write each act. Make sure that every student has a part to read and that the play has ample sound effects. When the class is ready, have students present the play, tape-recording it so that they can hear and critique it later.

Travel in Time

Virginia Hamilton's trilogy, *Justice and Her Brothers, Dustland,* and *The Gathering,* is about children with special powers that allow them to mind-travel into the future. Imagine that *you* had a time machine that gave you the power to travel in time. Would you go back in time? Would you go forward?

On the lines below, write a paragraph about one trip in your time machine. First name your destination and describe it. Then explain why you selected that place and what you did when you got there. Were there any special people you wanted to meet? Were there any special things you wanted to do or find out?

_____

_____

_____

_____

_____

_____

_____

_____

Justice and Her Brothers
Dustland
The Gathering
Virginia Hamilton

The Envelope, Please

    Virginia Hamilton's books have won many prizes for many reasons. Which of her books did you enjoy the most? Why do you think it deserves an award?

    Select any book by Virginia Hamilton that you especially enjoyed and create a literary prize for it. First, name your prize and list the qualities that a book needs to win. Then write a letter to Virginia Hamilton explaining why her book is getting the prize. In your letter, include specific examples from the book to show how it had the qualities the prize required. Finally, design your prize. It can be a medal, a ribbon, a scroll, or any form you want.

My literary prize is called _____.

To win this prize, a book must

1. _____

2. _____

3. _____

4. _____

Dear Ms. Hamilton:

_____

_____

_____

_____

                                                      Yours sincerely,

                                               _____

My award:

Arnold Lobel

(1936–1987)

"It is a kind of pleasant omnipotence that I feel at the drawing board," Arnold Lobel once remarked. "There is a little world at the end of my pencil. I am the stage director, the costume designer, the man who pulls the curtain." Lobel first discovered the power of his pencil as a sickly little boy who was raised by his grandparents after his parents' divorce. Frequent hospitalizations separated him from his classmates. To gain their friendship, Lobel entertained his classmates with stories, which he illustrated on the blackboard.

The allure of text and pictures continued into Lobel's adolescence, as he eagerly

Arnold Lobel

devoured children's books. After high school, he enrolled in New York City's Pratt Institute to further his training in illustration. At Pratt he fell in love with fellow artist Anita Kempler, a native of Cracow, Poland, and they married soon after their graduation in 1955. Lobel worked as an artist for a number of years, unable to sell his own book ideas. He had met with fifty publishers before

Harper commissioned him in 1961 to illustrate a picture book, *Red Tag Comes Back.* The following year he wrote and illustrated *A Zoo for Mister Muster.* He once claimed that his decision to write as well as illustrate children's books was simply a matter of earning 10 percent royalties rather than 5 percent, but he genuinely enjoyed both phases of book production.

During his career, Lobel produced or collaborated on more than eighty books for children, including three Caldecott Honor Books, *Frog and Toad Are Friends,* *Hildilid's Night,* *Fables,* and a Newbery Honor Book, *Frog and Toad Together.* He is especially well known for his "Frog and Toad" series. In the later years of their marriage, Arnold and Anita Lobel began to work together. Among the most successful of their collaborations is the richly designed alphabet book *On Market Street* (1981), which melded Arnold's writing with Anita's paintings.

A Zoo for Mister Muster. Harper, 1962.

Prince Bertram the Bad. Harper, 1963.

A Holiday for Mister Muster. Harper, 1963.

Lucille. Harper, 1964.

The Bears of the Air. Harper, 1965.

Martha, the Movie Mouse. Harper, 1966.

The Great Blueness and Other Predicaments. Harper, 1968.

Frog and Toad Are Friends. Harper, 1970.

The Ice-Cream Cone Coot. *Parents'* Magazine Press, 1971.

Frog and Toad Together. Harper, 1972.

Mouse Tales. Harper, 1972.

The Man Who Took the Indoors Out. Harper, 1974.

Owl at Home. Harper, 1975.

Fables. Harper, 1980.

The Book of Pigericks: Pig Limericks. Harper, 1983.

ALL ABOUT THE BOOKS

A Zoo for Mister Muster shows the animals coming to Mister Muster's home, but returning to the zoo when Mister Muster becomes a zookeeper.

Prince Bertram the Bad describes how a naughty prince is transformed into a good one.

A Holiday for Mister Muster tells about how Mister Muster takes the animals who have been ill with colds to the ocean.

Lucille is about a horse who yearns to be a lady.

The Bears of the Air tells of four little bears who want to have fun instead of completing the useful activities their grandfather favors.

Martha, the Movie Mouse is a "rags to riches" verse story of a mouse who finds a home (a movie theater) and a friend.

The Great Blueness and Other Predicaments explains the origin of colors.

Frog and Toad Are Friends, a 1971 Caldecott Honor Book, explores the value of friendship.

The Ice-Cream Cone Coot has comical verses that tell how various objects are transformed into birds.

Frog and Toad Together contains five more insightful tales of friendship.

Mouse Tales contains tales told by a father mouse to his seven sons as bedtime stories. Stories are illustrated with imaginative page borders.

The Man Who Took the Indoors Out is about a man who invites all his indoor things outside. They flee, but come home the following winter.

Owl at Home follows the format of the "Frog and Toad" books.

Fables is a collection of modern fables with engaging animal characters.

The Book of Pigericks: Pig Limericks contains amusing limericks illustrated with elaborately dressed pigs.

ACTIVITIES

Othericks! Read Lobel's *The Book of Pigericks: Pig Limericks* to students. Then discuss several examples of "pigericks," helping students to see that a limerick is a short, funny rhyming poem. Tell students that a limerick has five lines, and that the rhyme scheme is often *aabba.* Use a drumstick or your hand to tap out the rhythm. Lead students to realize that most limericks have three strong beats in lines one, two, and five, and two strong beats in lines three and four. Remind students that the purpose of a limerick is to make people laugh. Explain that limericks can be on any subject at all, not just pigs. Have students work in small groups to write a limerick about an animal of their choice. Older students may wish to capture the rhyme and rhythm of a true limerick, while younger ones might prefer to write funny five-line poems. Circulate among the students to offer help as needed. When all groups have finished, have them read their poems aloud.

Friendship Share Lobel's *Frog and Toad Are Friends* with the class. Then ask students to generate a list of words to complete this sentence: A friend is _____. List the suggestions on the chalkboard and explore various ways that friends show they care. Then have students form a "friendship circle" by sitting in a circle and linking hands. Join the circle yourself. One at a time, have each student turn to the person next to him or her and say something complimentary, such as "I like the way you share the crayons" or "You have a very pretty outfit on today." To complete the lesson, teach students the traditional friendship song: "Make new friends, but keep the old; one is silver and the other gold." Squeeze the hand of the student to your right and have him or her pass it down until everyone has had a "friendship squeeze."

Frog? Toad? Lobel is especially famous for his "Frog and Toad" series. As a science project, have students read encyclopedia entries or science books on frogs and toads to learn how to distinguish between the two creatures. Then have students create a chart to compare and contrast the animals. Students can divide their charts in half, writing "Frog" on one side and "Toad" on the other. Have students begin each side with a picture of the appropriate creature, then list its characteristics. Students might also want to bring in ceramic frogs and toads, or live ones, if they can, to share.

I Would Be a . . .

In *Prince Bertram the Bad,* the prince turns into a dragon when he hits the witch with a slingshot. Imagine that you were turned into an animal. What animal would it be? On the line below, write the name of the animal you would become. Then draw a picture of that animal.

I would be turned into _____.

Prince Bertram the Bad
Arnold Lobel

The Great Blueness

The Great Blueness and Other Predicaments explains how colors came to be. In the book, blue makes everyone sad, yellow hurts everyone's eyes, and red makes everyone angry. Finally, the wizard makes a mistake and creates all the colors.

In the spaces below, follow the color chart to make the colors you need to complete the rainbow. You will need red, blue, and yellow paint. Then use only one color to make a picture that describes how you feel today.

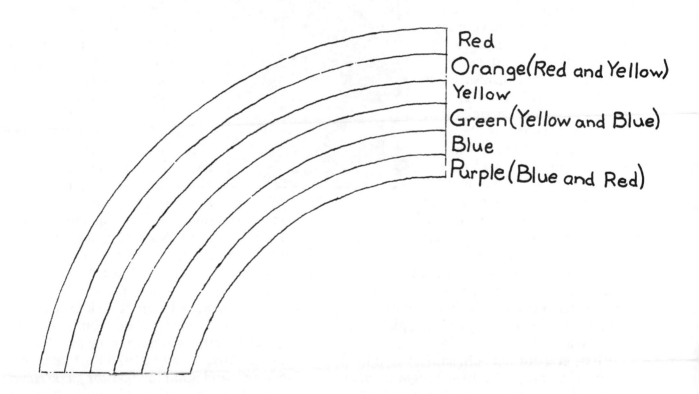

Red
Orange (Red and Yellow)
Yellow
Green (Yellow and Blue)
Blue
Purple (Blue and Red)

Today I feel _____.

The Great Blueness and Other Predicaments
Arnold Lobel

Katherine Paterson

(BORN 1932)

Born in China to missionary parents, Katherine Womeldorf Paterson spoke Chinese before she knew English. Her youth was spent shuttling between China and America; by the time she graduated from King College in Tennessee, Paterson had attended more than a dozen different schools. Small for her age and very shy, Paterson was further singled out for ridicule by her American classmates for her British accent and castoff clothing salvaged from a missionary barrel. Many years later, she recalled how as a lonely little first-grader she had returned home from school on February 14 without a single valentine. Her mother, grieving over her daughter's isolation, asked her why she didn't write a story about the incident. "But, Mother," Paterson replied, "*all* my stories are about the time I didn't get any valentines." A self-described "weird little kid," Paterson credits the library with supplying her with what little happiness she enjoyed as a child.

Katherine Paterson

After receiving her A.B. summa cum laude from King College, Paterson taught briefly in a rural Virginia elementary school before earning her master's degree in Christian education. Soon after, she conquered her fear and hatred of the Japanese—whom she had known only as enemy soldiers in her childhood—and traveled to Japan to follow in her parents' footsteps. She genuinely enjoyed her four years of missionary work among the Japanese, finding a true kinship of spirit with the people and a new way of looking at her world. Deciding to further her religious education, Paterson then accepted a fellowship at Union Theological Seminary, where she met and married John Paterson, a Presbyterian minister. The couple settled in Maryland, where their family soon included two birth sons and two adopted daughters, one Chinese, one Apache. Paterson's growing family sparked her literary creativity—she began writing when she was pregnant with her first son and awaiting the arrival of her first daughter from a Hong Kong orphanage. Without even a desk of her own, Paterson stole spare minutes from the tumult of her bustling house to try her hand at fiction. Nine years later in 1973, her first novel, *The Sign of the Chrysanthemum,* was published.

Although she finds writing difficult, Paterson has proved a prolific, skillful, and justly celebrated author. She is one of only a handful of authors to have twice won the Newbery Medal, first in 1978 for *Bridge to Terabithia* and again in 1981 for *Jacob Have I Loved.* "I have learned," she notes, "for all my failings and limitations, that when I am willing to give myself away in a book, readers will respond by giving themselves away as well, and the book that I labored over so long becomes in our mutual giving something far richer and more powerful than I could ever have imagined."

The Sign of the Chrysanthemum. Crowell, 1973.

Of Nightingales That Weep. Crowell, 1974.

The Master Puppeteer. Crowell, 1976.

Bridge to Terabithia. Crowell, 1977.

The Great Gilly Hopkins. Crowell, 1978.

Angels and Other Strangers: Family Christmas Stories.
 Crowell, 1979.

Jacob Have I Loved. Crowell, 1980.

Rebels of the Heavenly Kingdom. Lodestar, 1983.

Come Sing, Jimmy Jo. Lodestar, 1985.

ALL ABOUT THE BOOKS

The Sign of the Chrysanthemum tells of thirteen-year-old Muna's determination to find his warrior father. Although Muna never finds his father, his encounters with the wily samurai Takanobu and the principled swordmaker Fukuji help him gain self-esteem and maturity.

Of Nightingales That Weep tells how lovely, talented Takiko finds true happiness and love in war-torn medieval Japan.

The Master Puppeteer, set in eighteenth-century Japan, describes how thirteen-year-old Jiro runs away from his home in Osaka to become an apprentice at a puppet theater. Jiro finds his place in the world with the help of Kinshi, the puppetmaster's son.

Bridge to Terabithia describes how two fifth-graders, Jess Aarons and Leslie Burke, become close friends and together create Terabithia, a secret woodland kingdom. Leslie's death by drowning brings Jess great sorrow but also maturity.

The Great Gilly Hopkins is about plucky Galadriel Hopkins, a young girl abandoned by her mother. Through the affection of her foster mother Maime Trotter, Gilly realizes that "doing good on a tough job" makes a person happy.

Angels and Other Strangers: Family Christmas Stories has nine stories that reflect Paterson's concern for the world's lost and lonely.

Jacob Have I Loved traces how Sara Louise Bradshaw comes to terms with her bitter jealousy toward her twin, Caroline. In so doing, Sara realizes her own worth and others' appreciation of it.

Rebels of the Heavenly Kingdom, set during the mid-nineteenth-century revolt against the corrupt Manchu rulers, is an adventure story centering on the romance of Wang Lee and Mei Lin.

Come Sing, Jimmy Jo is the story of a gifted mountain boy, James Johnson, who becomes a country-music star. He comes to see that along with the gift of song, he is blessed with selflessness, strength, and wisdom.

ACTIVITIES

You're the Star! James Johnson in *Come Sing, Jimmy Jo* enjoys singing country and gospel music for an audience. Have your students stage a class variety show. Those who like to perform can sing, act, dance, or deliver a serious or comic monologue. Students might also want to write and present group skits and acts. Those who don't want to perform can participate in lighting, scenery, props, costumes, and publicity (including programs and posters). If students wish, they can invite other classes, administrators, parents, and community members to enjoy their show.

What Happens Next? Have the class read *The Great Gilly Hopkins* and write their own sequel to Gilly's story. Ask students to consider what Gilly's life might be like in the future. Will she learn to love her grandmother as she previously learned to love Mrs. Trotter? As students write, encourage them to consider such literary elements as setting, point of view, characterization, and humor.

Come to Terabithia Suggest that students work in small groups to create scale models of Terabithia. Have all students begin by locating specific details in the novel that describe Jess and Leslie's "secret land across the creek." Invite younger students to come and see the models. Individual class members might want to read relevant passages from the novel to the visitors.

All the World's a Stage Have students research the art of puppet making and puppet-show production. Then, as Jiro does in *The Master Puppeteer*, have the class perform a puppet show. Begin by dividing the class into groups to write the script, make puppets, and stage the performance. You might want to share the final production with other classes.

Once upon a Time . . .

Katherine Paterson began writing stories when her husband asked her to create a Christmas tale he could use in his work as a minister. Now it's your turn. On the lines below, write a story about any holiday you like.

Begin by deciding which holiday you want to write about. It might be Halloween, Thanksgiving, the Fourth of July, or any other holiday you choose. Then ask yourself, Who will read my story? Will they be my classmates? My friends? Younger children? Next, think about why you are writing your story—Am I writing to entertain, or to teach a lesson? Finally, brainstorm a list of characters and events, and you're on your way!

When you finish writing your story, you might want to draw pictures to illustrate it. You might also want to exchange your story with a friend.

_____

_____

_____

_____

_____

_____

_____

**Angels and Other Strangers:
Family Christmas Stories**
Katherine Paterson

48

Get the Scoop!

Imagine that the editor of your school newspaper has asked you to interview Katherine Paterson about her experiences in China. What things do you think your readers might want to know about China and Paterson's life there? What questions would you like to ask her?

Begin by reading about China in an encyclopedia or other reference book. Then jot down some notes about China's history, people, geography, culture, language, foods, and economy. Finally, write on the spaces below questions you would like to ask Katherine Paterson during your interview.

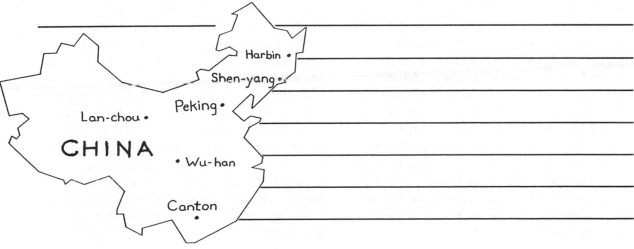

Bill Peet

(BORN 1915)

Drawing was Bill Peet's hobby from the time he was old enough to hold a crayon. "This hobby was especially handy in the wintertime after the first snows had turned to sleet and slush and sledding and the snowball wars had become impossible," he recalls. "I drew just about anything that came to mind, all sorts of animals (including dragons), trains, fire engines, racing cars, airplanes, gladiators, pioneers fighting Indians, World War I battles, Revolutionary War battles, football games, prizefights, or what have you." As you would expect from someone with Peet's talent and interest, the time allocated for drawing in art class proved insufficient. Somehow, he vowed, his hobby would become his profession.

Bill Peet

After graduating from high school, he won a scholarship to the John Herron Art Institute in his hometown, Indianapolis. After he completed art school, Peet realized that he had to find a way to make a steady living. Complicating matters was his determination to marry Margaret Brunst. He was thrilled to secure a job with an Ohio greeting card company, but his delight soon wore off when they assigned him the task of drawing flowers on sympathy cards. He headed west, seeking work in the film industry. He was soon hired to design storyboards. He sent for Margaret, and they married.

In the 1930s, Peet took what he assumed would be a temporary job with Disney Studios. More than twenty years passed, however, before he tried to break away by attempting to publish a picture book, *The Luckiest One of All.* It was rejected by every publisher he approached (in 1982, it became his twenty-seventh book). In 1959, Houghton Mifflin accepted *Hubert's Hair-Raising Adventure;* five years and four books later, Peet left Disney to become a full-time free-lance illustrator and children's book writer.

His interest in writing began while he worked in the motion-picture industry. "I began to think in terms of writing and as the years passed contributed more and more ideas to the motion picture stories," he noted. His screenplays a success, Peet began to turn his attention to children's books. As his enthusiastic readers and many literary awards demonstrate, Peet's books are as successful as his screenplays.

Reflecting on his career, Bill Peet remarked, "So my early ambition to illustrate animal stories was finally realized, and a little bit more, since I had never considered writing one. This way I can write about things I like to draw, which makes it more fun than work." And he still carries a tablet around with him and sneaks a drawing in now and again!

Ella. Houghton Mifflin, 1964.

Kermit the Hermit. Houghton Mifflin, 1965.

The Whingdingdilly. Houghton Mifflin, 1970.

The Caboose Who Got Loose. Houghton Mifflin, 1971.

How Droofus the Dragon Lost His Head. Houghton Mifflin, 1971.

Cyrus, the Unsinkable Sea Serpent. Houghton Mifflin, 1975.

Pamela Camel. Houghton Mifflin, 1984.

The Kweeks of Kookatumdee. Houghton Mifflin, 1985.

Bill Peet: An Autobiography. Houghton Mifflin, 1989.

Cock-a-Doodle Dudley. Houghton Mifflin, 1990.

ALL ABOUT THE BOOKS

Ella, the star elephant in the circus, hides and is left behind when the circus leaves town. She discovers that her new life is not what she anticipated.

Kermit the Hermit is a greedy crab who learns a valuable lesson about needing help and helping others.

The Whingdingdilly tells how Scamp, unhappy about being a dog, becomes even more unhappy when a witch changes him into a "whingdingdilly." Scamp realizes that he should have been satisfied with being himself.

The Caboose Who Got Loose is a rhyming story about how Katy Caboose gets her wish not to be the last car in the train.

How Droofus the Dragon Lost His Head tells how Droofus the Dragon survives when he is accidentally separated from his family. Things are fine until the king wants to have Droofus's head on the castle wall. Droofus uses his head instead of losing it.

Cyrus, the Unsinkable Sea Serpent, is challenged by a shark to wreck a ship and eat its passengers. He changes his mind and twice rescues a ship, first from a fierce storm and then from marauding pirates.

The Kweeks of Kookatumdee, related in verse, is about the flightless birdlike Kweeks, who are stuck on the tiny island of Kookatumdee. A frantic free-for-all existence is created by a food shortage on the island. In the end the Kweeks learn to fly to neighboring islands, where they find scores of ploppa trees, the trees that bear the fruit they depend on for food.

Pamela Camel, dissatisfied with her role in the circus menagerie of wild animals, runs away. She sees a train about to ride broken railroad tracks and risks her life to prevent injury to others. When the circus owners hear of her heroism, they take her back and make her the star of the circus.

Bill Peet: An Autobiography, a 1990 Caldecott Honor Book, is Bill Peet's own story told in words and pictures. Peet illustrates not only his own life but also events of this century, such as Lindbergh's historic flight and the Hindenburg disaster.

Cock-a-Doodle Dudley tells how the jealous goose Gunther drives the rooster Dudley into the woods to prove that roosters do not make the sun rise. The sun, who favors Dudley, stays hidden so as not to embarrass him.

ACTIVITIES

The Big Top Share Peet's *Pamela Camel* with students. Then discuss different aspects of the circus, beginning with Pamela's initial role in the wild animal menagerie and her later debut as the star act. Brainstorm a list of attractions students associate with the circus: clowns, tumblers, special foods, dramatic music, and so forth. Then have students design their own circus or carnival for younger students or special needs students, or to raise money for a school project or charity. The hosts of the student circus can make ringtoss or fishing games, perform as clowns and tumblers, paint faces, juggle, prepare and sell food, sing, and play musical instruments. "The Big Top" can be held in the classroom, in the school lobby, or in an outdoor courtyard.

Where in the World? Bill Peet's books are set in many different places. *Kermit the Hermit* takes place by the sea; *The Whingdingdilly* is set on a farm; *The Caboose Who Got Loose* is in a train yard; *How Droofus the Dragon Lost His Head* is in a castle. After students have read several of Peet's books and discussed the settings, invite them to create a mural or montage of the different settings they read about. Start with a wide roll of brown paper. Then arrange students into small groups and assign each group a different section of the mural. As students draw, paint, or color, have them refer to the books to locate details to include in their section. Students may want to try to emulate Peet's cartoon style or work in their own individual ways. After students have completed the mural, you might want to display it in a prominent place and arrange several of Peet's books in front of it.

My Poem Bill Peet enjoys using verse in a number of his books, such as *The Caboose Who Got Loose* and *The Kweeks of Kookatumdee*. Students might also enjoy experimenting with poetic form and writing a poem centered around the subject they know best—themselves! To give students a framework around which to anchor their verse, have them complete the following pattern:

Line 1—Direct students to write their first name.

Line 2—Invite students to list four words that describe themselves.

Line 3—Have students complete this sentence: "Who feels . . ."

Line 4—Ask students to complete this sentence: "Who needs . . ."

Line 5—Guide students to complete this sentence: "Who gives . . ."

Line 6—Tell students to write their address.

Line 7—Ask students to write their last name.

When all students have finished writing, have them share their poems with the class. They might want to read their poems aloud, exchange papers with a friend, or compile a class book.

Pantomime a Tale Select any Bill Peet story to read to your students. *Cyrus, the Unsinkable Sea Serpent* or *The Caboose Who Got Loose* will work especially well for this activity. Begin by defining "pantomime" for students. Stress that since mime is silent, facial expressions, gestures, and body language are very important. Tell students that you are now going to read a Bill Peet story and they are going to help you by pantomiming the action. As you read the story, have volunteers pantomime the action. You can select one student for each role, have students change roles with every page you read, or proceed in any way that suits the number of students and their grade level. You might also want to extend this activity by having a small group of students act out another Bill Peet story for the class, without reading from it or even telling the class the title. When the actors have finished, ask the rest of the class to guess which story was described.

Things That Make Me Happy, Things That Make Me Sad

In *The Whingdingdilly*, Scamp is unhappy as a dog. He becomes even more unhappy, though, when a witch changes him into a "whingdingdilly." What things make you happy? What things make you sad?

On the lines below, write five things that make you happy and five things that make you sad.

Things That Make Me Happy

1. _____

2. _____

3. _____

4. _____

5. _____

Things That Make Me Sad

1. _____

2. _____

3. _____

4. _____

5. _____

The Whingdingdilly
Bill Peet

Keep in Touch!

The Kweeks of Kookatumdee learn to fly. They leave Kookatumdec and go to a new island, with plenty of ploppa trees. The Kweeks might send a postcard back to their friends on Kookatumdee.

Imagine you were on a vacation and sent a postcard home to your friend. What would you say? First draw the picture on the front of the postcard. Then write a note to your friend. Don't forget to include your friend's address!

FRONT

BACK

The Kweeks of Kookatumdee
Bill Peet

Cynthia Rylant

[RYE-LUNT] (BORN 1954)

It took Cynthia Rylant many years to realize how deeply her childhood affected her writing. From the time she was four until she was eight, Rylant was raised by her maternal grandparents in Cool Ridge, West Virginia. Although her grandparents had little money, they enjoyed what Rylant calls a "rich existence." "They both possessed a quiet dignity and they did not complain about life," she has noted. "They lived life with strength, great calm, a real sense of what it means to be devoted to and responsible for other people." She realized with pleasure that the tone of her work reflects the simplicity of her grandparents' language and, at the same time, the depth of their hearts. To honor her heritage, she took her grandfather's last name, "Rylant," as her pen name.

Cynthia Rylant

When Rylant was eight, she left her grandparents and moved with her mother to Beaver, West Virginia. Although she was popular in school and an "A" student, Rylant always felt that she was on the outside of events. "I couldn't wait to get out of town when I grew up," she notes, "but I owe it everything." In other words, Beaver was a painful growing time that fed her writing later. When she was eighteen, she entered Morris Harvey College (now the University of Charleston), where she "sort of ignited in freshman English." "I loved everything I read," she remembers, "but I certainly never imagined that I could be a writer. I always felt inferior to my friends who wrote poetry and short stories. Always felt my life had been too limited. Nothing to write about."

When Rylant was twenty-two years old, the year after she earned her B.A., two extraordinary things happened to make her realize that she did indeed have talent and something to write about. First, she read children's literature for the first time and it astonished her. Second, she read James Agee's *A Death in the Family* and *Let Us Now Praise Famous Men.* She recognized in Agee's voice something of her own; he wrote about impoverished families in Appalachia. One night, she sat down and wrote *When I Was Young in the Mountains.* She mailed the manuscript to E. P. Dutton, a New York publisher, and it sold. She notes, however, that it wasn't until she had published seven books that she felt like a writer!

"I come from people who worked very, very hard and whose lives were never simple nor easy," she stresses. "In my books I try to touch on how hard life can be sometimes, but always, *always* show that for everything we lose, we will get something back."

When I Was Young in the Mountains. Dutton, 1982.

Miss Maggie. Dutton, 1983.

Waiting to Waltz: A Childhood. Bradbury, 1984.

Every Living Thing. Bradbury, 1985.

The Relatives Came. Bradbury, 1985.

A Fine White Dust. Bradbury, 1986.

Night in the Country. Bradbury, 1986.

Henry and Mudge in Puddle Trouble. Bradbury, 1987.

Henry and Mudge in the Green Time. Bradbury, 1987.

Henry and Mudge Under the Yellow Moon. Bradbury, 1987.

Henry and Mudge in the Sparkle Days. Bradbury, 1988.

A Couple of Kooks: And Other Stories About Love. Franklin Watts, 1990.

Henry and Mudge and the Happy Cat. Macmillan, 1990.

The Soda Jerk. Franklin Watts, 1990.

Henry and Mudge and the Bedtime Thumps. Macmillan, 1991.

ALL ABOUT THE BOOKS

When I Was Young in the Mountains, a Caldecott Honor Book, describes the simple everyday pleasures in the life of an eight-year-old girl and her younger brother, who live with their grandparents in Appalachia.

Miss Maggie tells about how a lonely boy named Nat is afraid of Miss Maggie, an old lady alone in her deteriorating house, until she needs his help. He then discovers that she is lonely and afraid, too.

Waiting to Waltz: A Childhood concerns growing up in Appalachia.

Every Living Thing contains twelve short stories about people whose lives are changed by their relationships with animals.

The Relatives Came tells about a family's joyous celebration with relatives who come from Virginia.

A Fine White Dust, a 1987 Newbery Honor Book, tells how thirteen-year-old Pete Cassidy reconciles his religious beliefs with his parents' different ones after a traumatic experience with a preacher.

Night in the Country celebrates the tranquil beauty of nature by capturing the sounds and sensations of a dark country night.

Henry and Mudge in the Green Time chronicles the charming adventures of Henry and his dog, Mudge. In this volume, Henry is stung by a bee and Mudge takes a bath.

Henry and Mudge Under the Yellow Moon continues the saga of Henry and his oversized pooch, Mudge.

Henry and Mudge in the Sparkle Days describes Henry's life with his dog, Mudge.

A Couple of Kooks: And Other Stories About Love contains eight short stories that sample the vast range of interesting things that can happen when ordinary people are drawn to each other.

Henry and Mudge in Puddle Trouble shows how Henry and his dog celebrate spring. The pair finds an early March flower that is good enough to eat, an April puddle to splash in, and a litter of kittens that Mudge adopts.

The Soda Jerk, written from the point of view of the soda jerk in a small town, is a free-verse portrait of small-town life.

Henry and Mudge and the Bedtime Thump recalls a time when Grandmother banished Mudge to the outdoors, leaving Henry alone and afraid at bedtime in Grandmother's unfamiliar house.

Henry and Mudge and the Happy Cat tells how Henry's family adopts a scraggly cat that instantly adopts Mudge—until the cat's owner comes to claim it.

ACTIVITIES

Sounds all Around Rylant's *Night in the Country* describes the swooping of the owls, the singing of the frogs, and the other sounds we hear as nature settles down for the night. Help students compare and contrast the sounds they hear outside in nature to those they hear inside a building. Begin by taking students outside for a brief walk. As they walk around, have them talk about the sounds they hear and then write what each sound is—the cry of a bird or the honking of horns, for example. Then come back into the classroom and repeat the process, having students list the sounds they hear now. In this instance, they may hear the scraping of chairs on the floor, the rasping of the loudspeaker, or the snap of a shade rolling up. When all students have discussed and recorded the sounds they heard outside and inside, make one big class chart on sounds. On one side, write the "outside" sounds students volunteer; on the other, the "inside" sounds they suggest. Display the chart in a prominent place.

Night Owls Read Rylant's *Night in the Country* aloud to the class. Then discuss some of the animals that are awake at night while we sleep: owls, raccoons, beavers, opossums, and frogs, for example. Take students to the library to learn about other nocturnal animals. Then have students work in small groups to assemble information about one or more of these creatures. Suggest that students include a description of each animal and its habits. For example, they might also mention the animal's diet, life cycle, and predators. When all students have completed their work, have each group present its findings in the form of a panel discussion.

A Is for Aardvark Rylant's *Every Living Thing* is a series of tales that tell how people changed as a result of their relationships with animals. There is no doubt that animals influence our lives very much. To explore the influence animals have had on students, construct a class alphabet book based around animals. Assign each student a letter; if you have more than twenty-six students, have pairs work together as necessary; if you have fewer than twenty-six students, assign some students more than one letter. Direct students to represent each letter of the alphabet with an animal whose name starts with that letter, as in *B* for "bat" or *M* for "monkey." Younger students can use more common animals, such as cats and dogs; older students can seek out less familiar creatures, such as lemurs and aardvarks. Tell students to devote one page to each letter. On each page, have students create an illustration with the animal and the letter in an action situation. Bind the book and share it with the class.

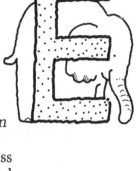

Down by the Bay Henry and Mudge, like other Rylant characters, have many amusing adventures. In *Henry and Mudge in the Green Time*, for example, Henry pretends to be king of a hill. Have students create an entire silly song with a silly song refrain. The class song can be centered around students' own adventures, or be created for the audience's amusement.

The refrain song "Down by the Bay" is suitable for students of all ages. If students do not make up their own refrain for their class song, they can use the "Down by the Bay" refrain. The refrain goes: "Down by the bay, down by the bay, where the watermelons grow, where the watermelons grow, back to my home, back to my home, I shall not go, I shall not go, for if I do, for if I do, my mother will say, my mother will say . . ." At this point, have students insert their own silly adventure lines, beginning with the words: "Did you ever see a . . ." Sample silly refrains include: "Did you ever see a whale with a polka-dotted tail?" and "Did you ever see a mouse cleaning her house?" After singing two verses, students sing the refrain "down by the bay," or their own refrain, and continue creating new verses for the song. Write down the entire song on the board so students can enjoy it again.

When I Was Younger . . .

Cynthia Rylant's book *When I Was Young in the Mountains* tells about the pleasure an eight-year-old girl has living in Appalachia. For example, she likes her supper of steaming corn bread, pinto beans, and fried okra, a vegetable. She enjoys going to the swimming hole, pumping well water into a tin bucket for her bath, shelling beans at night on the porch, and drinking sweet milk at the general store.

Can you remember the things that you used to do when you were younger? Are they different than the things you do now? Are they things you have outgrown?

Write six sentences beginning "When I Was Younger . . . ." As you write, try to use all five senses: taste, smell, touch, hearing, and sight.

1. **When I Was Younger . . .** _____

_____

2. **When I Was Younger . . .** _____

_____

3. **When I Was Younger . . .** _____

_____

4. **When I Was Younger . . .** _____

_____

5. **When I Was Younger . . .** _____

_____

6. **When I Was Younger . . .** _____

_____

When I Was Young in the Mountains
Cynthia Rylant

Celebrate the Season!

Cynthia Rylant's *Henry and Mudge in Puddle Trouble* tells how Henry and his dog Mudge celebrate spring. They find a flower that's good enough to eat, a puddle to splash in, and a litter of kittens.

Pick any season—winter, spring, summer, fall. Imagine you were a small child outside for the day. You can be alone, or have a pet or a friend with you. On the lines below, describe how you would celebrate the season.

_____

_____

_____

_____

_____

_____

_____

_____

_____

_____

_____

_____

Henry and Mudge in Puddle Trouble
Cynthia Rylant

Maurice Sendak

(BORN 1928)

"I was miserable as a kid," Maurice Sendak recalls. "I couldn't make friends. I couldn't play stoopball terrific, I couldn't skate great. I stayed home and drew pictures." His isolation was partly caused by his frail health, worsened by bouts with measles, pneumonia, and scarlet fever. The family's frequent moves added to the problem. He became an observer rather than a participant, capturing the world around him on his sketch pad. While still a child, Sendak decided to devote his life to writing and illustrating books. He and his brother Jack often made their own storybooks, combining comics or photographs clipped from newspapers with drawings they had made of other family members. He also recalls with great delight listening to his father's "beautiful, imaginative tales." These long stories, he believes, were the first important sources of his work.

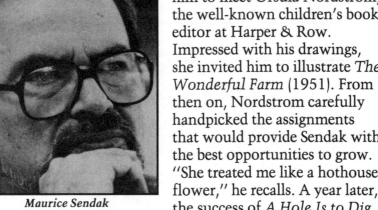

Maurice Sendak

His entry into the world of professional book illustration came about in a curious way. In 1948, while out of work, Sendak designed a line of animated toys with his brother. They took their designs to the famous New York toy store, F. A. O. Schwarz. Although the company felt the toys would be too expensive to mass-produce, they hired Sendak to design their window displays. Working at the toy store also gave Sendak the chance to browse through the children's book department, where he studied the great book illustrations from the past. The most important things that happened to Sendak at Schwarz, however, was that the store's book buyer arranged for him to meet Ursula Nordstrom, the well-known children's book editor at Harper & Row. Impressed with his drawings, she invited him to illustrate *The Wonderful Farm* (1951). From then on, Nordstrom carefully handpicked the assignments that would provide Sendak with the best opportunities to grow. "She treated me like a hothouse flower," he recalls. A year later, the success of *A Hole Is to Dig* enabled Sendak to become a full-time freelance illustrator.

One of Sendak's most famous characters is Rosie, who made her first appearance in 1960 in *The Sign on Rosie's Door*. In 1975, Sendak made the character a star in her own animated musical special, *Really Rosie;* in 1978, he transformed the work into a play. His most controversial book, *Where the Wild Things Are*, was awarded the Caldecott Medal in 1964. In his acceptance speech, Sendak noted that the "truth and passion" of his work come from the "awful vulnerability of children and their struggle to make themselves King of All Wild Things."

SELECTED WORKS BY
MAURICE SENDAK

Kenny's Window. Harper, 1956.

Very Far Away. Harper, 1957.

The Sign on Rosie's Door. Harper, 1960.

Nutshell Library (contains four miniature books: *Alligators All Around, Chicken Soup with Rice, One Was Johnny, Pierre)* Harper, 1962.

Where the Wild Things Are. Harper, 1963.

Higglety Pigglety Pop! Or, There Must Be More to Life. Harper, 1967.

In the Night Kitchen. Harper, 1970.

Outside Over There. Harper, 1981.

The Nutcracker. Harper, 1984.

The Love for Three Oranges. Harper, 1984.

In Grandpa's House. Harper, 1985.

Hector Protector And As I Went Over the Water. Harper, 1990.

ALL ABOUT THE BOOKS

Kenny's Window, the first book Sendak wrote, tells of a young boy who awakens from a dream in which a rooster asks him seven riddles.

Very Far Away tells about Martin who runs away when he feels neglected.

The Sign on Rosie's Door features brash and likable Rosie, who lures her friends into fantasies to escape boring summer afternoons.

Chicken Soup with Rice, a volume in *Nutshell Library*, is a book of rhymes about the months of the year.

Where the Wild Things Are tells how Max, sent to his room without supper, fantasizes that he travels to the land of the Wild Things and becomes their king. After his fantasy, he finds that his mother has supper waiting.

Hector Protector And As I Went Over the Water adapts two nursery rhymes for a tribute to Randolph Caldecott.

Higglety Pigglety Pop! Or, There Must Be More to Life, from a nineteenth-century nursery rhyme, memorializes Sendak's beloved terrier Jennie.

In the Night Kitchen tells the joyous story of Mickey falling from sleep into the Night Kitchen. He escapes and lands back in his bed.

Outside Over There, a picture book, is a story of sibling rivalry in which Ida, a young girl, rescues her sister from goblins.

The Nutcracker is an illustrated version of the ballet.

The Love for Three Oranges chronicles the collaboration of Sendak and Frank Corsaro on a 1982 stage production of Prokofiev's work.

In Grandpa's House, written by Sendak's father Philip, has two parts: a description of Philip's childhood, and a dreamlike story of a young boy who lives in a Jewish ghetto in Europe.

ACTIVITIES

A Cover Quilt Maurice Sendak has illustrated over seventy books written by other authors and written and illustrated more than seventeen books of his own. Create a class quilt of Sendak's books. Every time students read one of Sendak's books, have them design a cover for the work on a piece of construction paper. Direct them to include the title, author, and a picture they think represents the book and will make other students want to read it. Each time a new quilt square is completed, staple it to the existing quilt. Post the quilt in a conspicuous place on the bulletin board. Urge students to stop by and look at the quilt for other Sendak books they might like to read.

Who Am I? Many of Sendak's characters are well known—Rosie, Max, Jennie, and the Wild Things, for example. Play a literary guessing game by having students impersonate some of Sendak's best-known characters. Invite students to select any one of Sendak's characters. Have them each write the character's name on a slip of paper and fold the paper. Then collect all the slips and put them in a box. Ask the first student to pick a name from the box. Give the student a few minutes to recall everything he or she can about the character and to "slip into character." Then have the rest of the class ask yes and no questions to guess the character's identity. Students might begin with such questions as "Are you woolly?" "Are you bossy?" or "Are you funny?" The student who correctly guesses the character's identity gets to select the next slip of paper and impersonate the character on it.

Tenth Row Center! Rosie made her first appearance in 1960 in *The Sign on Rosie's Door.* Fifteen years later, she had her own television special; a few years after that, a play. Have students adapt any one of Sendak's books into a short play. First have the class together select a Sendak book that they especially liked. Then block out the play. Divide the class into groups. Have each group write dialogue and songs for their portion. When the groups have finished, rehearse the play and songs. Solicit volunteers to make scenery, assemble costumes, and do makeup, props, and publicity. Have students perform the play for other classes and parents. Ask the school's media department or a parent volunteer to videotape the performance so that students can watch it later.

Puzzle Mania Have students make jigsaw puzzles of favorite scenes from Sendak's work. Begin by giving each student a piece of stiff poster board. Working directly on the poster board, have students illustrate a favorite scene from Sendak's work. Suggest they make their pictures as detailed as possible. Then have students turn their pictures over and draw jigsaw puzzle shapes. If you wish, you can bring in shapes from real jigsaw puzzles for students to trace. Direct students to cut on the lines to create puzzle pieces. Students can exchange their puzzles with partners and see who can put together the puzzles first. Give everyone a bag in which to store the puzzle pieces.

Monster Alert

Maurice Sendak's Wild Things are shaggy monsters with pointy teeth. There are many different kinds of wild things: tall and short, fat and skinny, shaggy and smooth. You can draw a wild thing any way you want, even around a letter of the alphabet. The letter *C*, for example, might become an untamed C-serpent!

Pick any letter of the alphabet and turn it into a wild thing. In the space below your picture, write the name of your wild thing.

My wild thing is called _____.

Where the Wild Things Are
Maurice Sendak

66

A Name Becomes a Poem!

Draw a picture of any Maurice Sendak character you like, such as Rosie or Max. Along the left side of the page, write the letters in the character's name. For each letter, write a few words that describe the character. When you are finished writing, you'll have a poem about the character! A poem for Ida might look like this:

I think she was very brave fighting the goblins.

D on't you think so?

A close encounter!

_____

_____

_____

_____

_____

_____

_____

_____

_____

Dr. Seuss

Theodor Seuss Geisel

(1904–1991)

"You will never learn to draw, Theodor. Why don't you just skip this class for the rest of the term?" suggested Theodor Seuss Geisel's high school art teacher. Fortunately for readers around the world, the man who was to become "Dr. Seuss" ignored his teacher's advice.

Dr. Seuss

Geisel majored in English at Dartmouth College. As editor of the college humor magazine, Geisel published many cartoons centered around his now-familiar bizarre creatures. After graduating in 1925, Geisel entered Oxford University, intending to earn a Ph.D. in English. Noticing that Geisel doodled animals during lectures, classmate Helen Palmer suggested to him that he might be more interested in drawing than in literature. Geisel agreed with her advice, made her his manager, and a year later made her his wife. After a trip to Europe, Geisel began to draw successful cartoon ads for major corporations, including Standard Oil, Ford, and NBC Radio. Geisel first began to think of producing children's books after a humorous book he illustrated for Viking in 1931, *Boners*, sold well. He completed an alphabet book, but found no takers. Four years later he tried again. According to a famous story, he wrote *And to Think That I Saw It on Mulberry Street* on a transatlantic voyage. The numbing "da da *da* da da *dum* de *da de* de da" rhythm of the ship's engines provided the inspiration for the beat. However, he was unable to interest a publisher in the book, and gathered more than twenty-five rejection slips. One day he met a former Dartmouth classmate who had become the children's book editor for Vanguard Press. The editor was looking for a children's book, and Geisel had one to sell. *And to Think That I Saw It on Mulberry Street* was a hit on its publication in 1937, and "Dr. Seuss" was born. "Seuss" was his middle name, his mother's maiden name. His explanation for adding "Dr." is as follows: "I had been studying for a doctorate when I quit to become a cartoonist. My father had always wanted to see a Dr. in front of my name, so I attached it. I figured by doing that, I saved him about ten thousand dollars."

While all of Dr. Seuss's books have their admirers, the publication of *The Cat in the Hat* in 1957 marked a turning point in his career. Written in response to novelist John Hersey's criticism of the dull "Dick and Jane" primary-school readers, *The Cat in the Hat* resulted in the formation of Beginners Books, a series that revolutionized elementary-school readers. "I remember figuring I could knock it off in a week or so," he recalled, but it actually took nearly two years to write.

Dr. Seuss's books have sold more than eighty million copies altogether. When asked why he chose to write for children rather than adults, he replied, "I'd rather write for kids. They are more appreciative. Adults are obsolete children and the hell with them."

And to Think That I Saw It on Mulberry Street. Vanguard, 1937.

The 500 Hats of Bartholomew Cubbins. Vanguard, 1938.

The King's Stilts. Random House, 1939.

Horton Hatches the Egg. Random House, 1940.

McElligot's Pool. Random House, 1947.

Thidwick, The Big-Hearted Moose. Random House, 1948.

Bartholomew and the Oobleck. Random House, 1949.

If I Ran the Zoo. Random House, 1950.

On Beyond Zebra. Random House, 1955.

The Cat in the Hat. Random House, 1957.

How the Grinch Stole Christmas. Random House, 1957.

One Fish Two Fish Red Fish Blue Fish. Random House, 1960.

The Butter Battle Book. Random House, 1984.

Oh, the Places You'll Go! Random House, 1990.

ALL ABOUT THE BOOKS

And to Think That I Saw It on Mulberry Street describes how Marco creates a fantasy around the commonplace sights and sounds he encounters on his way home from school.

The 500 Hats of Bartholomew Cubbins features a king who requires his subjects to doff their hats in his presence. Bartholomew tries to meet this requirement, but hats magically appear on his head every time he removes one.

The King's Stilts argues that a kingdom works better when a king takes time off to play.

Horton Hatches the Egg, the first book in which Dr. Seuss uses sound repetition and rhyme, describes an elephant in a tree hatching an egg.

McElligot's Pool, a Caldecott Honor Book, marks the first time Dr. Seuss invents a new creature. Here, a child imagines a wonderful creature he can fish for in McElligot's pool.

Thidwick, the Big-Hearted Moose explains how Thidwick's hospitality is abused by his guests, who pile on his antlers. He escapes the hunters, but his rude guests end up as trophies on the Harvard Club wall.

Bartholomew and the Oobleck, a Caldecott Honor Book, shows how King Derwin mires his land in oobleck when he tires of other forms of precipitation. Bartholomew saves the day by telling the king to apologize.

If I Ran the Zoo, a Caldecott Honor Book, explains how Gerald McGrew dreams up fantastic animals for his imaginary zoo.

On Beyond Zebra is a series of letters beyond those in the alphabet.

The Cat in the Hat is an entertaining cat who wrecks the house with two children on a rainy day. Seeing the mother returning, the Cat in the Hat cleans up the mess, returning everything to normal.

How the Grinch Stole Christmas tells how the Grinch hates Christmas and tries to ruin it for the Whos of Whoville by stealing gifts and other material things.

One Fish Two Fish Red Fish Blue Fish uses a simple vocabulary and one new word per page to help very young children learn word recognition.

The Butter Battle Book is a serious satire on war. The "war" in this book is between characters who eat buttered bread either with the butter side up or with the butter side down.

Oh, the Places You'll Go! is a fantasy about growing up and all the things a child has to anticipate.

ACTIVITIES

You Can't Imagine What I Saw! *And to Think That I Saw It on Mulberry Street* describes both what Marco really sees and what he imagines he sees on his way home from school. First read the book to students. Then ask them to brainstorm a list of things they *really* saw on their way to school. Have volunteers share their lists with the class. Then ask students to write a paragraph that describes a scene more fantastic than the one Marco saw on Mulberry Street. Urge students to use their list of real items as a jumping-off point for their fantasies. Very young readers might want to tell their stories in pictures rather than in words. After everyone is finished, have students read their stories to the class. Decide which fantastic tale is the most fitting competition for Marco's whopper!

What's the Weather? In *Bartholomew and the Oobleck,* King Derwin tires of snow, fog, sunshine, and rain. He gathers his magicians to create a new form of precipitation, the gooey green oobleck. Share the book with your students as inspiration for a study of meteorology. Then divide the class into small groups to research and report on different aspects of the topic. Possible areas for study

include weather conditions, properties of the atmosphere, the history of meteorology, forecasting, climate, observation methods, and hurricanes and other weather phenomena. Students might also enjoy snipping weather forecasts from a newspaper and charting their accuracy over a week. After all the groups have completed their work, have them share their findings in the form of panel discussions. You might also want to set up permanent weather stations for continuously monitoring the weather outside, including a rain measurement station, a temperature chart, and a windsock.

Hats Off! Bartholomew Cubbins has 500 hats. Create a class hat collection by asking your students to design their own hats. Direct them to make the hat representative of their interests. A student who likes sports, for example, might decorate a hat with baseball cards, game ticket stubs, and other sports paraphernalia; a student interested in nature might use flowers, leaves, birds, and other natural objects. Students can use paper plates, newspapers folded into hat shapes, or real hats as the base for their personalized creations. After all students have finished their hats, hold a fashion show in which the students explain the meaning of the objects on their hats.

Math Magic In *Horton Hatches an Egg*, lazy Mayzie gets Horton the elephant to help hatch her egg. Horton sticks to his task because he is "faithful one hundred percent." Use this phrase as the basis of a mathematics lesson in percentages. Use manipulatives such as a pie, loaf, or other whole that can be divided to have students demonstrate 25 percent, 50 percent, 75 percent, and 100 percent. Then explain how 25 percent is the same as 1/4, 50 percent the same as 1/2, 75 percent the same as 3/4, and 100 percent the same as 4/4. Continue with the lesson, drawing finer distinctions (10 percent, 20 percent, etc.) depending on students' grade level and abilities. Finally, have students demonstrate their understanding of percentages by making a pie out of paper and dividing it by percentages.

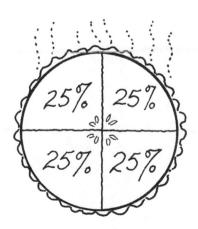

The Places I'll Go!

Dr. Seuss tells about growing up in *Oh, the Places You'll Go!* He talks about all the good things waiting for you as you grow up.

On the line below, draw a picture that shows one good thing that can happen to you at each age.

AGE
13

AGE
16

AGE
21

AGE
25

AGE
40

AGE
50

AGE
75

Oh, the Places You'll Go!
Dr. Seuss

Let's Eat!

Gerald McGrew in *If I Ran the Zoo* makes a super meal for an animal he calls a "natch." The meal is so good that the natch comes out of hiding to eat it. What food do you think is really good? A special sandwich? Spaghetti? Cookies? Write a recipe for making a dish that you like to eat. First list the ingredients and the kitchen tools you need. Then list the steps you have to follow to make this dish.

The food I am going to make is called _____.

The ingredients and kitchen tools are:

_____   _____

_____   _____

_____   _____

_____   _____

_____   _____

_____   _____

The steps are:

1. _____

2. _____

3. _____

4. _____

5. _____

6. _____

If I Ran the Zoo
Dr. Seuss

73

Chris Van Allsburg

(BORN 1949)

As a young child, Chris Van Allsburg's passion for art was so strong that it even collided with his physical health. "Once, in the second grade, I felt feverish at breakfast but concealed it from my mother because it was an art day. Midway through the morning art class, my teacher noticed that I looked a little green. . . . She took me out into the hall where we children left our coats and boots and asked if I felt O.K. I said I felt fine and then threw up into Billy Marcus's boots." By the time Van Allsburg was in the fourth grade, however, peer pressure influenced him to abandon his pen and paper in favor of more traditional male pursuits: baseball and football. "Kids who draw or wear white socks and bring violins to school on Wednesdays might have cooties," he explained.

Chris Van Allsburg

All through high school Van Allsburg assumed he would attend college to become an attorney, but through a bureaucratic error, he was accepted into art school at the University of Michigan. He was delighted by the mistake. "I thought it would be a great way to earn a college degree by goofing around for four years," he recalls. The university courses rekindled his early interest in art, however, and Van Allsburg soon found himself deeply immersed in sculpture, bronze casting, wood carving, and ceramics. After graduation he became a sculptor, drawing only as a hobby. A friend who illustrated books suggested to Van Allsburg that he try his hand at a children's book. Van Allsburg's wife, an elementary school teacher, took the book to several publishers, who suggested further refinements. This book, published as *The Garden of Abdul Gasazi* in 1979, gained Van Allsburg wide acclaim in the field of children's literature, and his career as a writer and illustrator of children's books was launched.

While Van Allsburg experiments widely with different artistic styles and techniques in his illustrations, his books share one thing in common. As Alfred Hitchcock appeared briefly in all his movies and Al Hirschfeld hides his daughter Nina's name in many of his caricatures, so Van Allsburg has a signature element: all his books include Fritz, the small dog from *The Garden of Abdul Gasazi*. "It's a little game with me," Van Allsburg says. "I look forward to concealing him more and more, so that you might have to spend four or five hours looking for him." The depth of his art makes it likely that the time would be well spent!

The Garden of Abdul Gasazi. Houghton Mifflin, 1979.

Jumanji. Houghton Mifflin, 1981.

Ben's Dream. Houghton Mifflin, 1982.

The Wreck of the Zephyr. Houghton Mifflin, 1983.

The Mysteries of Harris Burdick. Houghton Mifflin, 1984.

The Polar Express. Houghton Mifflin, 1985.

The Stranger. Houghton Mifflin, 1986.

Two Bad Ants. Houghton Mifflin, 1988.

Just a Dream. Houghton Mifflin, 1990.

ALL ABOUT THE BOOKS

The Garden of Abdul Gasazi tells how a little boy named Alan encounters the magician Abdul Gasazi while searching for a runaway dog named Fritz. The magician convinces Alan that he has turned Fritz into a duck. Miss Hester, Fritz's owner, tells Alan it was a trick. The reappearance of Alan's hat suggests the reality of the experience.

Jumanji, the winner of the 1982 Caldecott Medal, tells how two restless children, Judy and Peter, play a board game called Jumanji. The game becomes three-dimensional and lions, monkeys, and other wild creatures rampage through the house. When Judy wins, the game returns to its two-dimensional state.

Ben's Dream is about a boy who dreams that his house is floating— with him in it—through a flooded world. In the dream, he floats past his classmate Margaret. The dream ends with George Washington awakening Ben, and Margaret appearing at Ben's window to tell him of *her* identical dream.

The Wreck of the Zephyr is a frame story about a boy stranded during a storm on a strange island where boats sail above the water. The boy sails home with the islanders' magical sails, but his triumphant landing fails when a wind shift causes him to crash. No one believes the boy's tale, and he devotes his life to trying to find the island again.

The Mysteries of Harris Burdick is a collection of fourteen black-and-white illustrations prefaced by the mysterious story of Harris Burdick. The loosely connected scenes challenge readers to create their own story around them.

The Polar Express, winner of the 1986 Caldecott Medal, follows a young boy seeking Santa to the North Pole on Christmas Eve. The boy gets a bell from Santa's sleigh. On the trip home, he loses the bell; but the next morning, he finds it in a box under his family's Christmas tree. The bell rings beautifully, audible only to the boy and his sister.

The Stranger explains how Mr. Bailey, a farmer, accidentally runs over a mute stranger with his truck and brings him home to recover. While the stranger stays with the Baileys, winter turns to summer. When the stranger leaves, winter returns. Every year after that, winter comes a week late to the Bailey farm, and "See you next fall" appears on their windows.

Two Bad Ants tells the story of two ants who leave the safety of the ant community to venture into a perilous kitchen.

Just a Dream tells how Walter, a litterbug, changes his ways after he dreams of a future destroyed by landfills as high as Mount Everest.

ACTIVITIES

You Go! Jumanji, from Van Allsburg's book of the same name, is a board game. The instructions explain that the game is "a young people's jungle adventure designed especially for the bored and restless." Have small groups of students design their own board games. First, have the groups brainstorm ideas for their games. Do they want their game to be two-dimensional, as in traditional board games and the beginning of Jumanji, or *three*-dimensional, as Jumanji becomes? Then have students decide on their game's motif and aim. For example, they might want to consider a game centered around the ocean, their school, or outer space. Allow students time to design and test their games. Make sure they include an instruction sheet that explains the steps in the game. When everyone is finished working, arrange the class so that each student has a chance to try all the games.

If This Is Tuesday . . . In *Ben's Dream*, Ben falls asleep while studying for his geography test. He dreams that his house is floating through a flooded world. Begin by reading *Ben's Dream* to your students. Then have them list all the great structures Ben passes: the Statue of Liberty, Big Ben, the Eiffel Tower, the Leaning Tower of Pisa, the Parthenon, the Sphinx, St. Basil's, the Great Wall of China, and Mount Rushmore. Using a large world map or globe, have students locate each structure and mark it with a push pin. Then have volunteers connect the push pins with a continuous piece of string, tracing Ben's route around the world. Next, arrange students in small groups. Assign each group one of the places Ben visits. Have students research the history of the place, its importance, and interesting facts about it. Suggest that students try to locate additional pictures, postcards, souvenirs, and other memorabilia related to their structure. After students have completed their work, have each group report its findings to the class. You might want to display the pictures and other artifacts in the classroom.

Come Sail with Me! *The Wreck of the Zephyr* describes a mysterious island where boats sail above the water. Invite students to construct their own boats and create a class flotilla. Begin by having students locate pictures of different kinds of boats in books, magazines, and newspapers. Discuss all the different types of boats (sailboats, paddleboats, steamships, etc.) and then have students design their own boats out of paper, wood, or found objects. When all the students have completed their boats, have each student explain the type of boat he or she created and its capabilities. Finally, gather the boats into a class fleet and create a display.

Create Your Own Story *The Mysteries of Harris Burdick* has fourteen pictures accompanied only by titles and brief captions. Show the book to your students, reading the titles and captions. Then have students write a short story that ties together the fourteen illustrations. Since the pictures can appeal to preschoolers as well as students in the upper grades, you can adapt this activity for younger students by having groups create a story to tell orally, rather than requiring a written story of each student.

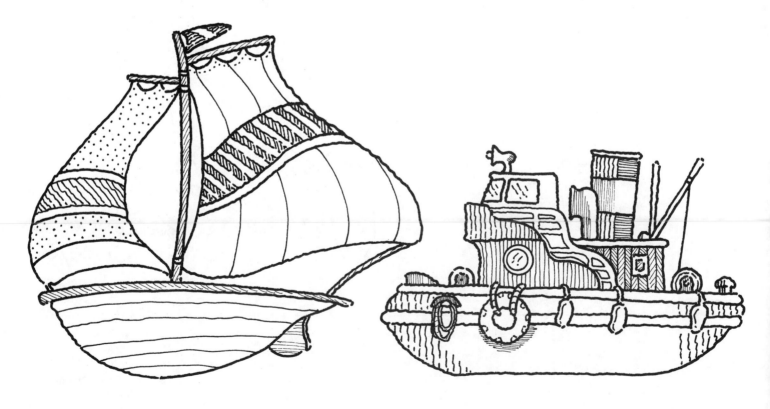

Around the World in Eighty Days

In *Ben's Dream*, Ben dreams that he floats in his house through a flooded world and sees the world's great structures. Imagine that *you* had a chance to travel around the world. Where would you go? What things would you most like to see?

On the world map below, trace your route around the world. Then write a letter home explaining what places, people, or things you visited and why you wanted to see them. What was your most special memory of your trip around the world?

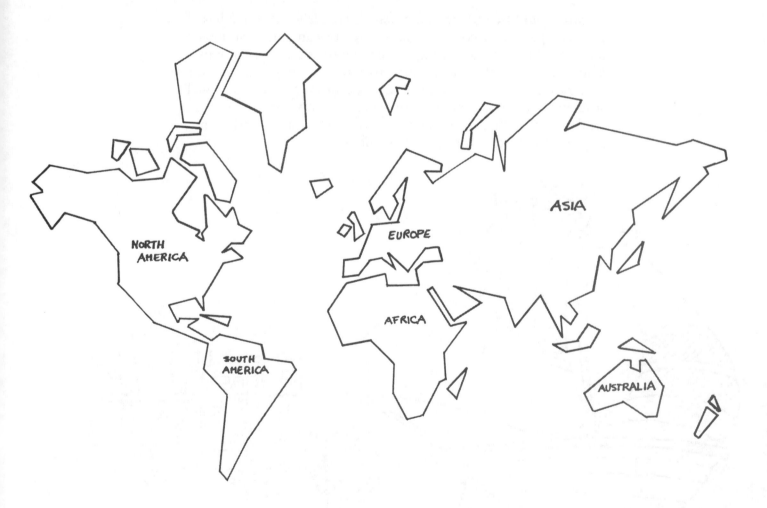

Ben's Dream
Chris Van Allsburg

If I Could Help the World, I Would . . .

In *Just a Dream,* Walter stops being a litterbug after he dreams of the world being destroyed by trash.

Imagine that *you* had Walter's dream. After you woke up, you also wanted to help make the world a better place. In the spaces below, list five things you could do to make the world better for everyone. Then circle the thing you think would be the most helpful. In the lines provided, explain why it is your first choice.

The ways I could help improve the world are:

1. _____   3. _____

2. _____   4. _____

5. _____

_____ is my first choice because _____

_____

_____

_____

_____

_____

Just a Dream
Chris Van Allsburg

79

Laura Ingalls Wilder

(1867–1957)

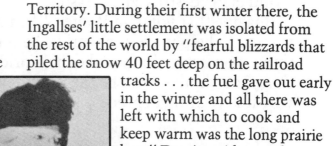

"Once upon a time, sixty years ago, a little girl lived in the Big Woods of Wisconsin, in a little gray house made of logs." So begins Laura Ingalls Wilder's *Little House in the Big Woods*, the first of her eight books that chronicle frontier life in the late nineteenth century. Wilder was a sixty-five-year-old Missouri homemaker when she began the "Little House" series. By the time she completed the series eleven years later, she had become one of the most beloved and acclaimed young adult writers of the twentieth century.

Laura Ingalls Wilder

"When to my surprise the book made such a success and children all over the U.S. wrote to me begging for more stories," she later remarked, "I began to think what a wonderful childhood I had had. How I had seen the whole frontier, the woods, the Indian country of the great plains, the frontier towns, the building of railroads in wild, unsettled country, homesteading and farmers coming to take possession." Laura was accustomed early to pioneer life, for soon after her first birthday, her parents continued their restless trek across the country. After a brief stay in Missouri, the Ingallses headed west, to Kansas and Indian territory. Soon after, they returned to Wisconsin and by 1874 had homesteaded on the banks of Plum Creek, in Minnesota. When a plague of grasshoppers devoured the crops, plunging the family into ruin, they decided to help run a hotel in Burr Oak, Iowa. When Laura was ten, the family returned to Walnut Grove. Finances became more strained, and Laura baby-sat to help. Seeking to reverse his fortune, Mr. Ingalls became a storekeeper with the railroad in De Smet, Dakota Territory. During their first winter there, the Ingallses' little settlement was isolated from the rest of the world by "fearful blizzards that piled the snow 40 feet deep on the railroad tracks . . . the fuel gave out early in the winter and all there was left with which to cook and keep warm was the long prairie hay." Despite widespread famine, the Ingallses survived. To help her parents send her blind sister Mary to a special school, Laura found a teaching position.

Despite her misgivings about farming, Laura married neighboring farmer Almanzo Wilder in 1885 when the school year ended. Her doubts proved prophetic, for within two years the young couple endured the failure of their crops, the death of their infant son, Almanzo's paralysis from diphtheria, and the destruction of their home by fire. The only bright spot in these early years was the birth of their daughter Rose in 1886. The Wilders moved to Missouri, bought a farm, and began to raise crops and livestock. To supplement the family income, Laura became the poultry editor for the *St. Louis Star*.

Wilder went to San Francisco to solicit the help of her well-published daughter in making the transition from writing articles to writing fiction. Soon thereafter, Wilder sold *Little House in the Big Woods*, and her career was launched. Wilder wrote her series, she explained, to help "children now to understand more about the beginning of things, to know what is behind the things they see—what it is that made America as they know it."

SELECTED WORKS BY
LAURA INGALLS WILDER

Little House in the Big Woods. Harper, 1932.

Farmer Boy. Harper, 1933.

Little House on the Prairie. Harper, 1935.

On the Banks of Plum Creek. Harper, 1937.

By the Shores of Silver Lake. Harper, 1939.

The Long Winter. Harper, 1940.

Little Town on the Prairie. Harper, 1941.

These Happy Golden Years. Harper, 1943.

The First Four Years. Harper, 1971.

ALL ABOUT THE BOOKS

Little House in the Big Woods describes Wilder's life as a young child in the Wisconsin woods. Pa supports his family by hunting, trapping, and farming. At night, Pa plays his fiddle and sings to his family.

Farmer Boy, the only book in the series not focused on the Ingallses, describes Almanzo Wilder's childhood on a flourishing New York farm.

Little House on the Prairie chronicles the family's travels from Wisconsin to Oklahoma. The family is happy in Oklahoma, but they must move when the Indians assert their rightful claim to the land.

On the Banks of Plum Creek describes how the Ingallses' idyllic existence is shattered when hordes of grasshoppers destroy their wheat crops and drive them off the land.

By the Shores of Silver Lake takes up with the family when they are deeply in debt and struggling to cope with Mary's blindness. In an effort to improve his fortunes, Pa goes to the Dakota Territory to work in a railroad camp. After he settles, he sends for his family and together they try to carve out an existence.

The Long Winter recalls the brutal winter in De Smet, when fierce blizzards blocked the arrival of the supply trains and many suffered from starvation. Almanzo and his brother greatly help the others when they locate and distribute wheat that a farmer had saved for seed.

Little Town on the Prairie picks up the story of the Ingallses after the long, hard winter. The residents of De Smet joyfully celebrate their survival with church socials, dances, and "literaries." Now a young lady, Laura attracts the attention of the dashing Almanzo Wilder, who courts her.

These Happy Golden Years tells how Laura, not yet sixteen, takes a job teaching school. Although she is miserable in the drafty shanty with her unwilling pupils, she endures for Mary's sake. She welcomes the arrival of Almanzo every Friday to take her home to her family.

The First Four Years describes the hardships and the joys of Laura and Almanzo's early married years.

ACTIVITIES

Travel with the Ingallses Working from a large present-day map of the United States, have students locate the places mentioned in the "Little House" books you are using. Then show students a map of the United States in the 1860s, when Wilder began her travels. Have students compare the two maps to show how the country has changed. Discuss the reasons the Ingallses might have picked such places as the Big Woods of Wisconsin (ample game to hunt for food and trap for furs, enough wood for housing and heat, fertile soil for farming, plenty of privacy); Plum Creek, Minnesota (the promise of "free land" to homestead); and Burr Oak, Iowa (a chance to educate the children amid a thriving community). Students should understand that the primary lure of the West was the promise of free land and a chance to make a fresh start.

Education a Hundred Years Ago On the chalkboard, have students chart what they think might be some differences in education between the 1890s and today. Their charts can look like this:

	1890s	**Today**
Subject Matter	grammar	foreign languages
	penmanship	sciences and math
Classroom	all grades together	students arranged by ages
	no central heat	comfortable rooms
Teachers	no married women	married women
Methods of Learning	memorization	concepts

Then conduct a brief lesson in nineteenth-century style, emphasizing choral response, strict attention, and rote memorization.

Time Capsule The "Little House" books preserve a way of life that has vanished. Arrange students in small groups and have them list ten items they would put in a time capsule to preserve their way of life for future generations. After each group has completed its list, share their work to come up with one list of ten or more items. If students wish, gather the ten items and create a time capsule. Bury the capsule with an appropriate ceremony and publicity.

Give a Gift Wilder and her family endured great hardships, although they shared much love and mutual support. Tell students they have the power to go back in time to give young Laura any gift they wish. Have them write brief descriptions to share with the class. You may wish to turn this into a community service project, as students help others in different ways.

Are We There Yet?

Imagine that like Laura Ingalls Wilder, you and your family are going to move across the country. The Ingallses traveled in a covered wagon; you're going by automobile or camper.

First think about the way the country is today, and decide where you want to move and why. Consider such factors as friends and family in the region, job opportunities, cost of living, topography, and weather. Then use the write-on lines below to tell where in the country you would most like you and your family to live. Explain your reasons.

_____

_____

_____

_____

_____

_____

_____

_____

_____

_____

_____

_____

_____

_____

_____

_____

_____

_____

All the Way Home

What a life Laura Ingalls Wilder had! With her family, she traveled all around the frontier—from Wisconsin's Big Woods to the wild Dakota Territory. Her travels continued after she married, too.

We've jumbled up the events of her life. Arrange them in the correct order along the time line. Next to each event, draw a picture that shows what you think her life was like at that time.

1890   Laura, Almanzo, and Rose move to Westville, Florida.

1885   Laura Ingalls marries Almanzo James Wilder, August 25.

1876   The Ingallses move to Burr Oak, Iowa.

1892   The Wilders return to De Smet.

1874   The Ingallses move to Walnut Grove, Minnesota.

1886   Rose Wilder born, December 9.

1868   The Ingallses move to Missouri.

1879   The Ingallses move to De Smet, South Dakota.

1894   The Wilders move to Mansfield, Missouri.

1869   The Ingallses move to Kansas.

Thumbs Up? Thumbs Down?

How do you decide if a book is worth reading? One good way is to read a review of the book. Newspapers, magazines, and other periodicals publish book reviews. In a book review, the writer describes the good and bad points of a book. It's your turn to review a book!

First list the things you look for in a good book. You might want to consider such things as interesting characters and an exciting story. Then pick a book and write your review. Begin with a plot summary, so that your reader knows what the book is about. Then compare your book with the things you look for in a good book, to decide whether you would recommend the book to someone else.

Things I look for when I read a book:

1. _____   3. _____

2. _____   4. _____

The book I am going to review is _____.

Book Review:

_____

_____

_____

_____

_____

_____

_____

_____

_____

_____

Dear . . .

Imagine that *you* are a character in one of your favorite books. You might be Jess Aarons in *Bridge to Terabithia* by Katherine Paterson, or Bill Everett in *Bill and Pete* by Tomie dePaola. Pretending to be the character in the book, write a note to another character in the book. If you were Jess, for instance, you might want to write to Leslie Burke. Before you begin writing your note, complete the questions below.

1. The character I picked is _____ from the book

_____.

2. I want to write to_____.

3. Here are several things I want to write about:

_____   _____

_____   _____

_____   _____

_____   _____

The things I've just listed are things that interest the character I am pretending to be. Now I'll write a note in my character's "voice."

My note:

Dear_____,

_____

_____

_____

_____

_____

_____

_____

                                                    Sincerely yours,

                                        _____

To Be Continued!

Have you ever wished the author of a book you really liked had written one more chapter? Here's your chance to write that new last chapter! First pick a book you liked. Then decide what you want to say in your new chapter. To gather ideas, think about characters, events, and places you want to include. Write your chapter on the lines.

The book I am going to write about is _____.

_____

_____

_____

_____

_____

_____

_____

_____

_____

_____

_____

_____

_____

_____

_____

You Ask the Questions!

Pretend that you are a newspaper reporter. "Get an interview with a character from your favorite book," barks your boss at the newspaper. Whom will you interview? Why did you select this character? What questions will you ask? Have a classmate pretend to be the character you selected. First prepare the questions you want to ask. Then interview the character, writing in the spaces provided below. Use quotation marks to show the dialogue between you and the character.

_____

_____

_____

_____

_____

_____

_____

_____

_____

_____

_____

_____

_____

_____

_____

_____

_____

_____

_____

Slip on a New Jacket!

Check out a new hardcover book! Look at the picture on the *book jacket*—the loose cover that wraps around—and read the description on the inside. That's what most people do before they decide whether or not to read a book! Here's your chance to make a book jacket that will make others want to read a book you liked. After you select the book you want to make a jacket for, write a brief summary of it for the inside front flap. Next, design a cover picture. You may also want to draw a picture of the author for the back cover or the back flap, and write a few sentences about the author's life and works.

Use the spaces below to design your book jacket. Do your finished design on a piece of paper that's large enough to wrap around the book. You may want to look carefully at several book jackets to see where the words and pictures go before you design your own jacket.

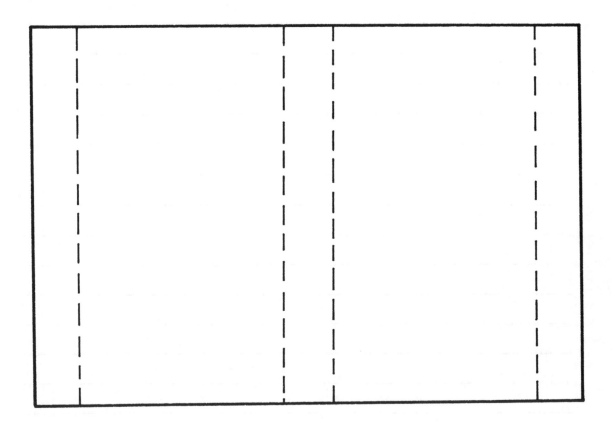

Star Struck

Here's your chance to be a star! Gather two or three of your classmates. Pick a book you all liked. Together, write a new scene for the book. Base your scene on the characters, action, and setting in the book. When you have finished writing, act out your scene for the rest of the class. Add costumes, scenery, and props, if you like.

We wrote this new scene for (book title) _____
by (author)_____ .

_____

_____

_____

_____

_____

_____

_____

_____

_____

_____

_____

_____

_____

_____

_____

_____

_____

Written by_____ _____ **Date**_____

_____ _____

Creating a Haiku

A haiku is a poem that has three lines. The first and third lines have five syllables each, and the second line has seven syllables. Haiku often use words that capture the five senses. The following haiku describes a storm:

The lightning flashes!
And slashing through the darkness
The night-herons screech.

— Basho, seventeenth century

Write a haiku describing your feelings about a book you liked. Brainstorm a list of ideas and then select the ideas you like the best. Write your brainstorming and final poem on the lines below. You might also want to draw a picture to go with your haiku.

Brainstorm of ideas

_____   _____

_____   _____

_____   _____

Haiku

_____

_____

_____

Buy This Book!

A publisher gave you a large budget to plan a book advertising campaign. Get together with several classmates to pick the book you want to sell. Then create a pie chart to show how you will spend your budget. What percentage will you spend on television and radio commercials, newspaper and magazine advertisements, author's book tours, billboards and posters? Finally, explain your pie chart to the class. Be prepared to give reasons for spending your money the way you are planning to. Are you advertising the book in a way that will reach the right audience?

Budget for Advertising Campaign

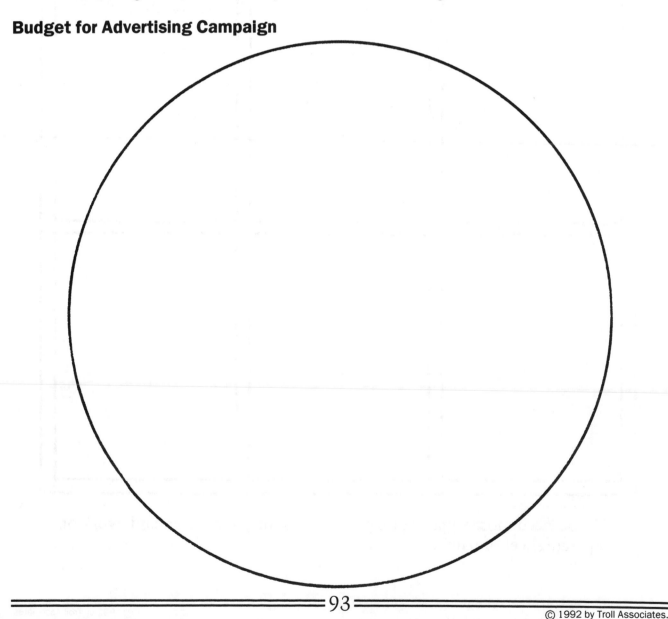

You've Got *Sixty Seconds!*

You're in charge of a book advertising campaign. First, decide what book you want to sell. Then plan a sixty-second television commercial. In the spaces below, prepare a *storyboard* for your commercial. A storyboard is like a comic strip; it has rows of squares with pictures in them that tell the story. Under each scene of your commercial, write the words your characters and announcer will say.

If you need more squares or bigger squares for your storyboard, work on a separate sheet of paper.

Stamp of Fame

Many famous authors have been honored by being placed on postage stamps. Decide what author you would honor in this way. Then create the stamp. Include a picture of the author, the author's birth date, some background objects that represent the author or his or her stories, and the stamp's value. Draw your stamp in the space below.

Who, What, Where, When, How, and Why

Evaluate a book you have read. Ask yourself these questions about the book: who, what, where, when, how, and why. Fill in the answers to the questions on the spaces provided below. Finally, based on your answers, write a few sentences explaining whether or not you would recommend the book.

Who is this book about?_____

What is this book about?_____

Where does the story take place?_____

When does the story take place?_____

How does the story end?_____

Why do things turn out the way they do?_____

I would/would not recommend this book because_____

_____

_____

_____

_____

WHO, WHAT, WHERE, WHEN, HOW, WHY?